James W. Moore

THE TOP TEN LIST FOR CHRISTIANS

Priorities for Faithful Living

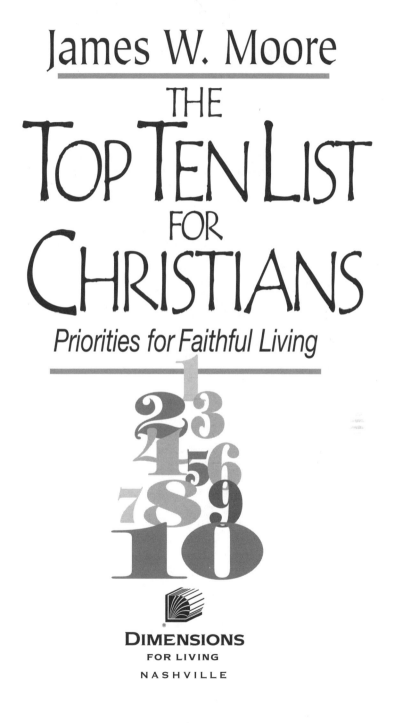

DIMENSIONS
FOR LIVING
NASHVILLE

THE TOP TEN LIST FOR CHRISTIANS
PRIORITIES FOR FAITHFUL LIVING

Copyright © 1999 by Dimensions for Living

This book is printed on recycled, acid-free, elemental-chlorine-free paper.

Library of Congress Cataloging-in-Publication Data

Moore, James W. (James Wendell), 1938–
    The top ten list for Christians : priorities for faithful living /
James W. Moore
        p.   cm.
    ISBN 0-687-97570-0 (alk. paper)
    1. Christian life—Methodist authors.   I. Title
BV4501.2.M58155   1999
248.4—dc21   99-11348
                                                                    CIP

01 02 03 04 05 06 07 08—10 9 8 7

MANUFACTURED IN THE UNITED STATES OF AMERICA

THE TOP TEN LIST
FOR CHRISTIANS

To

June

on the occasion

of our fortieth anniversary

CONTENTS

INTRODUCTION

he very mention of a Top Ten list these days would make most people think of David Letterman, and understandably so. Letterman made it popular: the Top Ten list. However, the truth is that Top Ten lists have been around for a long, long time.

Without question, the first and best Top Ten list is recorded in the book of Exodus. It's called the Ten Commandments, and that list is just as relevant today as it was in ancient times. Anyone who is awake enough to "smell the coffee" can easily see that life is better when we love God and other people; life is better when we respect our parents and tell the truth; life is better when we are honest, faithful, kind, and gracious in all our relationships. That's the way God meant it to be, and life works better for us when we live daily by these dependable spiritual laws, by this great Top Ten list.

Understanding that Top Ten lists can be helpful and that we all need help as we make our way through this world, I have put together in this book a "contemporary" Top Ten list for Christians. The best Top Ten list is obviously the Ten Commandments, but here is another list of Top Ten things to remember as we make our faith journey through this world.

I hope this list will enable us to remember the real priorities of life and encourage us to move into the future with faith, hope, love, joy, trust, and commitment so that we may live purposefully and celebratively as we embrace the exciting days ahead.

As you explore this Top Ten list, I'm sure you will think of others that could be added, and that is well and good. But for now, let me invite you to try these ten on for size.

Remember That

LOVE IS THE GREATEST!

Scripture: 1 Corinthians 13:1-13

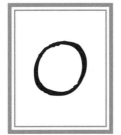

Our granddaughter Sarah is three and a half years old now. I know that this sounds like a proud grandfather talking, but it is true: She is a delightful child, with a vivid imagination. As you can imagine, she received many wonderful gifts this past Christmas, but without question her favorite gift was a videotape of the classic movie *The Wizard of Oz*. She absolutely loves that video, and watches it over and over and over.

And she identifies with the characters. She pretends to be Dorothy and assigns roles to all the other members of the family. Her dad is the Tin Man. Her mom is the Lion. Her grandmother is the Wizard. Her baby brother is Toto, the dog, and I am the Scarecrow.

You remember the story: Dorothy and her friends go down the yellow brick road to Emerald City to see the wizard of Oz. Dorothy wants the wizard to help her get back home to Kansas. And as you probably recall, the Lion wants the wizard to give him courage, the Tin Man wants a heart, and the Scarecrow thinks he doesn't have a brain, so he wants the wizard to give him a brain.

For at least five consecutive days over the Christmas holidays, Sarah called me "Scarecrow" and I called her "Dorothy." Each morning, Sarah would come into the den and say, "Good morning, Scarecrow. Do you have a brain today?" And I would answer, "No, not yet. But we are going to Emerald City to get me one!"

During that week, Sarah and I made lots of trips to the grocery store together. I would say to her, "Come on, Dorothy. We are going down the yellow brick road to Emerald City." She would run and put on her special shoes, and off we would go. When we arrived at the grocery store, I would tell her that the grocery cart was a magic carriage. She would jump in it, and we would do our shopping.

One morning at the checkout counter, Sarah, who was sitting in the cart, began helping me put the groceries on the counter. The cashier was impressed, and with a warm smile, she said to Sarah, "Aren't you nice to help?" To which Sarah said, "I have to help him because he doesn't have a brain."

The cashier looked—how shall I say this?—surprised at first, maybe even a little shocked, until I explained the context. When she understood the game we were playing, when she understood the specifics of the situation, when she understood clearly the context in which that statement was made, she joined in the game. She complimented Dorothy on her beautiful red shoes, and asked about the Lion and the Tin Man and Kansas—and Toto.

The point is clear: We can't fully understand what's going on; we can't fully comprehend what's being said; we can't fully grasp the meaning of a situation until we know the historical context. What is being said here? Who said it? Why is it being said? When is it being said? To whom is it being said? What was said just before it, and just after it? What were the concrete, specific, historical dynamics that produced these particular words in this unique situation?

It always helps to know the context in which something is said or written. This is uniquely true with Bible study. Look, for example, at 1 Corinthians 13, the "Love Chapter." The words here are beautiful enough to stand alone: "If I speak in the tongues of men and of angels, but have not love, I am a noisy gong or a clanging cymbal. And if I have . . . powers . . . to remove mountains, but have not love, I am nothing. . . . Love is patient and kind; love is not jealous or boastful; it is not arrogant or rude. . . . It is not irritable or resentful; . . . the greatest of [all] is love" (RSV).

These are powerful, moving words; timeless universal words. However, these incredible words (eloquent as they are) become even more powerful when we understand the context in which the apostle Paul wrote them. Paul wrote them to the Corinthian church when the church was in a big mess.

Paul had founded the church and stayed there with them for a time. As long as Paul was with them, all went well. But then Paul left, and problems erupted. Word came to Paul that the church was literally being torn apart by all kinds of problems—selfishness, jealousy, factions, cliques, immorality, political infighting, and lawsuits among the members. Hatred, hostility, and bitterness were running rampant and tearing the church apart.

Let me give you one graphic example to show you how bad off and mixed up the Corinthian church had become. You remember that in the early church, Holy Communion, the Lord's Supper, was a full meal. It was a time when the church came together as a family to celebrate God's love for them, and their love for God and each other; to celebrate God's goodness and generosity, and their oneness as God's children.

But look what had happened: It was absolutely unbelievable. Holy Communion wasn't holy in Corinth. It had become an ugly, spiteful battleground. Some members (out of spite) would rush to Communion and purposefully try to eat up all the food so that the latecomers (who weren't in their group) wouldn't get anything to eat. This was their cruel way of gigging those they didn't like! That's a sick spirit, isn't it? It is the exact opposite of what Holy Communion is all about. It is the exact opposite of what the Christian faith is all about.

Now, when the apostle Paul heard about what was going on, he got angry. He sat down and wrote them a series of letters, trying to straighten them out. Of course the crown jewel of that writing is found in 1 Corinthians 13. Paul spent twelve chapters exposing their sins, showing how ridiculous and unchristian they had been acting, and pointing out that what they were doing was not working.

And then he says, "Now let me show you a bet-

15

ter way" and bursts forth with the "Love Chapter." He tells them that irritability won't work; that jealousy and bitterness won't work; that arrogance, resentment, and choosing up sides won't work. He says to them: It doesn't matter how beautifully you can speak, it doesn't matter how smart you are, it doesn't even matter if you can do impressive, mind-boggling things; if you are not loving, none of it is worth anything.

He says to them: If you want to stay healthy as a Christian, if you want to be God's church, if you want to live in the spirit of Christ, then live the life of love. Make a new start with your life. Try this better way; make love your aim. Put love first. In every situation ask, What is the loving thing to do?

Paul's message in this text is so appropriate and relevant to our world today because the situation in our world today is so much like the situation in the Corinthian church back there in the first century. It makes me so sad to see so much selfishness, cynicism, litigation, immorality, abuse, and violence.

If the apostle Paul were here today, I know what he would say to our world, don't you? He would say: "Look, what you're doing is not working. Try a better way. Try the way of love."

Now, with all this as a backdrop for our thinking, let me underscore three ideas that remind us why love is indeed the greatest.

Love Is the Greatest Because It's Always Rooted in Gratitude

You may be wondering why all of a sudden (in a chapter on love) I'm talking about gratitude. The reason is captured in an old saying that goes like this: "Gratitude is the parent of all other virtues." I believe that. It's our gratitude that produces our faith, our hope, and our love.

Erma Bombeck was a great inspiration to me. Her wonderful way of looking at life with candor and humor delighted the hearts of people all over the world. Soon after she was diagnosed with the illness that eventually took her life, she wrote a wonderful column about gratitude, about seeing every day as a gift from God. She wrote: "Living tomorrows before they get here has become a full-time job for me, and I'm not going to do it anymore. It's the kind of society I live in. We have a curious need to know what the future is going to be."

Bombeck went on to describe how we exhaust ourselves worrying about the future, how we can't wait to know what the weather's going to be tomorrow, how we can't wait to find out what the sex of the baby we are carrying is going to be, and how we even make contractual provisions in case the marriage doesn't work. She pointed out that so many people get so busy arranging the future that they forget to live and celebrate the day. And then she concluded with these words: "Slowly, within the past year, I have found myself looking on each day as a gift. Think about it. In a life that has no guarantees, today is the only shot you have. It's yours. Free. No strings attached. Yours to see, to feel, to smell, to live, to celebrate, to share, and to appreciate."

You know what Erma Bombeck was saying in that article, don't you? She was saying, "This is the day that the LORD has made; let us rejoice and be glad in it" (Ps. 118:24). She was saying, It doesn't matter how eloquently we may speak, or how wise we may be, or how successful we may become, if we are not gratefully loving, it's not worth anything.

I don't know about you, but I have made up my mind: I'm going to be more grateful, because gratitude is the parent of all virtues, and love is deeply rooted in gratitude.

Love Is the Greatest Because It's Always Rooted
in Graciousness

Stephen Covey, author of the best-seller *The Seven Habits of Highly Effective People* (New York:

Simon & Schuster, 1990), tells about riding a subway in New York City one Sunday morning. He said people were sitting quietly in the car; some reading, others looking out the window. It was calm and peaceful. The only sound was the rhythmic rumbling of the subway.

Then the train stopped. Suddenly, a man and his children entered the subway car. The children were loud and rambunctious. Covey said that instantly the climate of the car changed. The father took a seat next to Covey and just put his head down and closed his eyes. The children were yelling back and forth, grabbing papers, and jumping on the seats. It was very disturbing.

Covey said he wondered how that father could be so insensitive to let his children just run wild like that. Everyone on the subway car was irritated. Finally, Covey said he just couldn't stand it anymore, so he turned to the man and said, "Sir, do you realize your children are disturbing a lot of people. I wonder if you couldn't control them a little more."

The father lifted his gaze and said, "Oh, you're right. I am so sorry. I guess I should do something about them, but I'm sort of at a loss right now. We just came from the hospital. Their mother died about an hour ago. I don't know what to do, and I guess they don't know how to handle it, either."

Covey wrote: "Can you imagine how I felt at that

19

moment? Everything changed in an instant. The way I looked at that man, the way I looked at those children changed instantly. Before, there was aggravation; now there was only love, compassion, sympathy, and understanding . . . because now I knew the truth of their hidden pain."

I don't know about you, but I've made up my mind: I'm going to be more gracious because I know that everybody has a hidden pain. I'm going to assume that everybody I meet has a burden that I can't see. So I'm going to be gentle with them and gracious to them. My prayer is that God, in his amazing grace, will enable us to be more grateful for that gift of each day and more gracious to everyone we see.

Love Is the Greatest Because It's Always Rooted in Generosity

Have you heard the story about the wealthy king from a mideastern country who came to America for an operation? The American surgeon was accustomed to setting prices by the patient's ability to pay, but he couldn't decide how much to charge His Royal Highness. Should it be $1,000 to be a good neighbor? Or $5,000 to match his usual fees? Or $10,000 to prove the operation was worth the trip? After all, a king is a king.

The doctor remembered that his minister had once been a missionary in the king's area of the world, so the surgeon called his minister and asked his advice. The minister said, "Oh, don't worry. The king is an honorable man like you. He understands value. Simply send him an invoice with no amount indicated and then add a handwritten note that says: 'The highly esteemed king will do the honorable thing.' "

The surgeon did just that. Back came a check for $75,000. The surgeon was overjoyed. He bought his wife a new outfit, bought a new car, and blew the rest on a cruise. When he returned home, he opened his mail. He found a letter from his minister. In it was a pledge card. At the bottom of the pledge card was a handwritten note from his pastor which read: "The highly esteemed church member will do the honorable thing."

Always and everywhere, the honorable thing is to be generous. Generous not just in our giving, but in our relationships with other people. Generous with our love, kindness, patience, understanding, and respect.

In another one of his letters, Paul said to "outdo one another in showing honor." In other words, be generously loving and respectful toward other people. I don't know about you, but I've made up my mind to be more grateful, more gracious, and

more generous, because these three signal qualities will make us more loving. Love is, after all,
the key sign of Christian discipleship.

A crucial thing to remember as we move forward in our faith journey through this world is
this: Love is the greatest!

Remember That

HOPE IS STILL ALIVE

Scripture: Luke 24:13-27

ave you ever noticed how much men just love the television remote control? Jerry Seinfeld, talking about this, once said, "Men don't just want to know what's on TV; they want to know what *else* is on TV."

I saw a greeting card recently that said: "What do you give a man who has everything? Answer: A second remote control."

I confess my guilt here. I love to channel surf with my remote control. I can channel surf with either hand, and sometimes with both hands at the same time! I am not a computer whiz, so I haven't learned how to surf the Net yet, but I can TV channel surf with the best of them.

Late one night recently, I was flipping through the cable TV channels when I hit upon the movie version of the great Broadway musical *Camelot*. It was the final scene, and I was captivated. I actually put the remote control down.

In *Camelot*, the final scene is indeed poignant and powerful. King Arthur sits alone in the forest. A lull has come in the battle. King Arthur sits there resting; but more than that, he is brooding, depressed, and heartsick. He is the picture of disillusionment. All of his hopes and dreams have been dashed. He is fighting a war against his most famous and trusted knight, Sir Lancelot.

Lancelot has betrayed him and stolen away the love of King Arthur's queen, the beautiful Guinevere. King Arthur's hopes that his kingdom can be one of peace, goodness, and unity have been devastated by the divisive actions of Lancelot. The dream of the Knights of the Round Table, where each one sat in equality, had been thrown for a loop by this war that pitted friend against friend.

So, here in this final scene, King Arthur sits all alone, so downhearted and discouraged, as he looks back over a life of great goals and noble ambitions now seemingly shattered and destroyed. Suddenly he hears a noise. Thinking it might be an enemy, he grabs his sword, only to discover a young boy approaching him, a boy no more than twelve or thirteen years of age. The boy is looking for King Arthur and immediately recognizes the famous king.

The boy tells King Arthur that he has come to join him in Camelot. From his earliest childhood, the boy says, he has heard of the Knights of the Round Table, how they honor and respect each other, how they work to protect the people, how their cause is good and true and noble. He wants to be like that, he says; he wants to be a Knight of the Round Table.

Suddenly King Arthur realizes that his dream has not died. The vision of yet a court of justice and equality, a land of right and truth, a people of nobility and integrity, the vision, the dream—it's still alive!

"Quick, boy, kneel," the king orders him. Taking the mighty sword, Excalibur, he places the flat blade on each of the boy's shoulders and then says to him in a loud and proud voice, "I dub thee, Sir John, Knight of the Round Table."

Then King Arthur lifts the young boy up and says, "Go back home, my son. Tell everyone that Camelot is possible. Run, Sir John, run! Tell the world it's still possible! Run, Sir John, run! Tell everyone that hope is still alive!"

25

What a moment! As I saw that powerful scene depicting so graphically the touching picture of a man who is down and out, brokenhearted, and disillusioned, but who suddenly has his hope restored—as I saw that, my mind flashed back to that moving passage in Luke 24 in which two followers of Jesus are trudging down the Emmaus Road. Their leader has been crucified. Like King Arthur, these two disciples are the painful portrait of the walking wounded when suddenly they get a new lease on life.

Remember the story with me: It is Easter afternoon. Cleopas and Simon have been followers of Jesus, but now they have thrown in the towel. They have quit, and they are limping down the Emmaus Road like broken and defeated warriors. They know about the Crucifixion; they saw it with their own eyes. But they do not yet know about the Resurrection. They have not yet experienced the risen Christ. Disappointed, disillusioned, defeated, heartbroken, downcast, they trudge down the Emmaus Road toward home. Their hopes for the future have been dashed; so, not knowing what else to do, they turn back toward the old life.

Picture them in your mind: Their shoulders are slumped. Their heads are bowed as though they carry on their backs a crushing burden of defeat and dejection. They limp along with weary steps as if their shoes were weighted with lead. Their eyes are misted over with the tears of disillusionment. They walk along in silence. They dare not speak for fear they will break into uncontrollable sobbing.

At last, with a sigh weighted with despair, the younger man speaks, "He's dead. He's gone. It's all over. They have killed him, and without him we are nothing. We should have known this wouldn't work. It was too good to be true, too idealistic for this cruel world. How could we have been such fools? We followed him. We trusted—we thought he was the one to save us, and now it's all over."

Now, that is the bold portrait of the stress-fractured spirit. Down, dejected, defeated, worn, weary, wounded.

But we also know that that is not the end of the story. No, the risen Lord comes to them. He walks with them. He talks with them. He opens the Scriptures to them. He breaks bread with them, and as they experience the resurrected Christ, they, too, get resurrected. They are healed. They find new life. And they rush (no more trudging, no more limping) back to Jerusalem to share the good news with the other disciples. They run shouting, "Hope is still alive, Christ is risen, Christ is alive!"

Isn't that a great story? There are so many powerful images and dramatic symbols here. It is packed full of the stuff of life. There are so many helpful lessons for us in this story. We could go in so many different directions. But for now, let me just lift up three special insights that underscore the good news here, the good news for people who suffer from a stress-fractured spirit. Ready? Here they are.

Lesson One: Christ Comes to Us in a Special Way When We Are Hurting

He is always with us in every circumstance of life, but over the years I have noticed that he seems to draw even closer to us when we are in pain. Cleopas and Simon were hurting that day as they plodded down the Emmaus Road. And then, suddenly, Christ was there with them to give them strength and meet their need. That's the way it works.

It seems like it would be easy for us to feel the presence of Christ with us when life is bright and beautiful and all the breaks are going our way, but the truth is that Christ is never nearer to us than when we are hurting. Time after time, I have heard people say, "This is the hardest thing we have ever gone through. Our hearts are broken, but we will be all right because God is with us as never before." Time and time again I have heard hurting people make that powerful statement: "God is with us as never before."

He is uniquely and especially with us when we are hurting, and I think I know two reasons why. First, I think it's because we are more open to the presence of God when we are down and out. And second, I believe that God is like a loving father who wants to be especially close to his children when they are in pain. Parents know what I'm talking about.

A few years ago when our daughter Jodi suddenly became ill, we couldn't get there fast enough. We wanted to be with her; we wanted to help her. God is like that. This is an important lesson that explodes out of this story in Luke 24. Christ comes to us in a special way when we are hurting.

Lesson Two: Christ Has the Power to Heal Our Hurts

In Luke 24 we see how the healing happens. Cleopas and Simon are trudging along with a stress-fractured spirit. But then Christ comes to them and walks with them, symbolizing the importance of the daily walk with Christ. He talks

29

with them, showing the power of prayer. He opens the Scriptures to them, underscoring the importance of Bible reading. He breaks bread with them, an obvious plug for Holy Communion. And he sends them back to the church.

Look at this: Prayer, Bible study, the Sacraments, staying close to the church, and the daily walk with Jesus Christ. Through these holy habits, Christ can bring healing to a fractured spirit.

In a *Peanuts* comic strip, Charlie Brown and Peppermint Patty are leaning against a tree on a beautiful spring day. Peppermint Patty says, "Chuck, what do you think security is?" Charlie Brown says, "Security? Security is sleeping in the backseat of the car when you're a little kid, and you've been somewhere with your mom and dad . . . and it's nighttime. You're riding in the car and you can sleep in the backseat and you don't have to worry about anything. Your mom and dad are in the front seat and they're doing all the worrying. They take care of everything."

Peppermint Patty smiles and says, "That's real neat!" But then Charlie Brown begins to get this serious look on his face and he raises his index finger and says, "But it doesn't last. It doesn't last. Suddenly, you're grown up and it can never be that way again. Suddenly, it's over—and you don't get to sleep in the backseat of the car anymore. Never!"

Peppermint Patty gets a sad and frightened look on her face and says, "Never?" Charlie Brown nods and says, "Never." Then stricken with the tough realities and the difficulties of life, Peppermint Patty says, "Hold my hand, Chuck! Hold my hand!"

The good news of the Christian faith is that we have someone to hold our hand. Jesus Christ came into the world to save us, to redeem us, to deliver us, to strengthen us, and to tell us that we are not alone, that we don't have to face the hard demands of life alone, that he is with us, holding our hand and healing our hurts.

Lesson Three: Christ Shares His Resurrection with Us

When we experience the risen Lord, we (like Cleopas and Simon) get resurrected, too. We get new life. This is one of the most amazing lessons of Easter. Christ was not the only one who got resurrected; the disciples got resurrected, too. After what they had seen on Good Friday, they were down for the count—devastated, defeated, disillusioned. But then came Easter. Christ breathed new life into them. He shared his resurrection with them.

Bishop Ellis Finger once told of a first-grade teacher who was having a horrible day. It had rained all day and thirty-seven first-graders had been cooped up in a small classroom. Having had no recess, the children were absolutely wild. The teacher could not get them calmed down. There had been one problem after another all day long, and the teacher was "beside herself" and even more anxious than the children were for the three o'clock bell to ring at the end of the school day.

At a quarter till three, the teacher noticed that it was still pouring outside, so she began the arduous task of getting the right raincoats, the right rainhats, and the right boots on the right children. Finally, she had them all ready to go home except for one little boy. He had a pair of boots that were just impossible to get on. No zippers, no snaps, no hooks, no buttons: They had to be pulled on with great effort. The teacher pushed and pulled, yanked and tugged, until finally they slipped on. She was so relieved.

But then the boy said, "Teacher, you know what? These boots ain't mine." The teacher wanted to scream, but she didn't. She said a quick prayer, took a deep breath, pushed the hair back out of her face, and began the difficult process of getting the boots back off the little boy. She pulled and jerked, yanked and tugged, until finally the boots came off. Then the little boy said, "They're my sister's, but she lets me wear 'em."

Now, the Resurrection is not ours. It belongs to

Christ, but he lets us wear it. And when we strap on the boots of Christ, when we take up his torch, when we commit ourselves to continue Christ's ministry of love, and when in faith we accept him as our Savior, then we become whole. Our stress fractures are healed; our hope is restored; and we really come alive.

NUMBER 8

Remember That

FAITH HAS ITS OWN TASTE TEST!

Scripture: Psalm 34:4-8

n his book *The Miracle of Love* (Old Tappan, N.J.: Fleming H. Revell, 1972), Charles Allen talks about how difficult it is to define the word *love*. He says it's like *honey*. You can't adequately define it or sufficiently describe it. You have to taste it. He puts it like this:

> Someone once asked me to define the word *honey*. I studied about it and finally came up with this definition: "Honey is a sweet, syrupy substance manufactured by bees." I realize that is a very inadequate definition. I know I cannot tell you what honey is. All I can do is give you some honey and let you taste it for yourself.

We know what Dr. Allen is talking about, don't we? Some things do indeed defy description. They are too big for words. To understand them, we have to experience them personally. We have to taste them. That is precisely what the psalmist is talking about in Psalm 34 when he says these classic and powerful words that have resounded throughout the ages: "O taste and see that the LORD is good" (v. 8). That was one of the first verses of Scripture I memorized as a little boy in Sunday school. It's interesting to note that when God created us, he gave us five senses:

We can see;
we can hear;
we can touch;
we can smell;
we can taste.

Now, in Psalm 34, the psalmist was very wise in his choice of words because the sense of taste is without question the most personal of the senses. When you taste something, you are personally involved with it. When you taste something, you experience it intimately because you receive it within. We can see something from a distance. We can hear something and tune out and let our minds wander. We can touch something reservedly. We can sniff around the edges of something, but taste requires a personal involvement. To taste something is to really take it in, to really experience it personally.

That's what the psalmist is underscoring for us here. It's not enough to just see the goodness of the Lord. It's not enough to just hear about it from others, or touch it fearfully, or catch a brief whiff of its fragrance. We need to *taste* and see that the Lord is good. Taste it for yourself. Don't just go by what others say. Taste it, savor it, relish it. Receive it within.

Let me ask you something, a question you and you alone can answer because it's so personal. Be honest, now. Have you tasted the Lord's goodness? Have you tasted it for yourself? Have you personally experienced God in your life? Have you really received him within? Do you on your own know Christ as Lord and Savior? We can ride on our parents' coattails or our friends' faith experiences only for so long. At some point, we have to seize our moment, take our plunge, experience our own leap of faith, make our own personal decision to welcome God into our lives. We have to taste the goodness of God for ourselves. Nobody else can do it for us.

Now, let me break this down a bit and bring it closer to home. Let me ask you three very specific and very personal questions:

Have You Tasted God's Redeeming Love?

Brian Bauknight tells the story of a man who was the president and CEO of a major corporation here in America. The man read a book that impressed him greatly. It was entitled *Sons and Daughters of God*. The man was so inspired by the book that he decided to order three hundred and fifty copies to give to the executives of his company. He wrote the publisher in Chicago, ordering the books. A few days later there came a computer reply that read, "Sorry, but we can't find three hundred and fifty *Sons and Daughters of God* in Chicago. Try Los Angeles!"

The single most important question of your life and mine is this: How do I become a son or daughter of God in my life's journey? The answer: By God's redeeming power.

Redemption is what the Christian gospel is all about. It is God's gracious ability through Christ to turn your life around, and God's gracious ability through Christ to take that which seems useless and make it usable; to take that which seems hopeless and make it hopeful; and to take that which seems defeated and make it victorious. That's what the cross is all about: God changing sadness to joy, despair to confidence, death to life. It's about God in Christ redeeming the situation, and a symbol of shame becoming a badge of triumph. The good news for today, the take-home-value for today, is this: God has the power and the desire to redeem your life and make it better. If you will let God, he will turn your life around.

Have you heard about the king who once owned a magnificent, large, perfect diamond? It was the pride of his empire. However, one day, under mysterious circumstances, the brilliant diamond was damaged. Its resplendent beauty was marred by a long, hairline scratch. The king was heartbroken. He sent word throughout the kingdom that he would give an enormous reward to anyone who could repair his diamond. No one came forward. All the best diamond cutters feared failure. Then, an artist appeared and offered to rescue the diamond. "Its greatest flaw shall be its most splendid glory," he announced confidently. He kept the diamond in his possession for many weeks, then he returned it to the king.

As the king unveiled his precious stone, he held his breath. Perhaps the artist's hand had slipped and the stone was now worthless. Perhaps the artist was a fraud and a scoundrel, or maybe even a robber. Slowly, carefully, the king unwrapped the diamond. When he finally caught a glimpse of his priceless treasure, it was so magnificent that it took his breath away. The king was absolutely delighted! The artist had performed the miracle of redemption, turning the hairline scratch into the long stem of an exquisite rose now carved delicately into the diamond. The diamond had been saved by the touch of the master's hand. That's the story of redemption. We can be changed like that, saved like that, redeemed like that—by the touch of our Master's hand.

Some years ago I saw a fascinating musical on one of our Methodist college campuses. It was called *For Heaven's Sake*, written by Helen Kromer. The play consisted of a series of vignettes designed to make us think seriously and deeply about our relationship with God and the church.

In one scene, a young man sings about the dramatic changes that have happened to him since he invited God into his life. He sings about how God is making him over—completely! He uses the analogy of a house and confesses that before God came into his life that the young man was like a small, modest bungalow in need of small repairs (a little rust here, a few leaks there), but basically life was comfortable in his little house. But God came in and went overboard, adding new foundations, adding several floors, multiplying chores, and talking repeatedly about how much better the place could be—and continuing to work away to improve it.

The song concludes with these poignant words: "God's making me over / I just can't be the same anymore." The song is about salvation, reconciliation, and redemption—how God can come in and turn our lives around and give us a new lease on life; how God in God's amazing grace can make us over.

Well, that's the first question. How did you do? Has God turned your life around? Have you tasted, really tasted God's redeeming love?

Have You Tasted God's Forgiving Love?

Some years ago, on a ranch in South Texas, an elderly woman was critically ill. She was at the point of death. All the family, the ranchhands, and the neighbors had gathered around her deathbed. Quietly, respectfully, they waited and watched. The doctors had told them the end was near and there was nothing else that could be done medically.

Suddenly there was a knock at the front door. It was a traveling revival preacher. He had arrived in the nearby town that morning, and someone had told him about how seriously ill the woman was. He had come right out to the ranch. He went to her bed and took hold of her hand. Weakly, she opened her eyes and said to him, "Who are you? I don't know you."

The revival preacher patted her hand and said, "They tell me that you don't have much time left. You are approaching death fast now, and I have come to forgive your sins and to get you ready to meet your Maker."

The elderly ranch woman suddenly sat up in bed and firmly said to the revival preacher, "Let me see your hands."

She took a quick look at his hands; then resolutely she said, "You, sir, are an imposter!"

"Pardon me?" answered the preacher.

"You, sir, are an imposter," she said a second time. She then added, "Only that one with nailprints in his hands can forgive my sins! Only that one with nailprints in his hands can get me ready to meet my Maker!"

Let me ask you something: Have you personally felt that forgiveness that comes only from him with nailprints in his hands? Have you tasted the redeeming love of God? Have you tasted for yourself God's forgiving love?

Have You Tasted God's Encouraging Love?

It's so easy to become discouraged in today's world. There are so many pressures, stresses, deadlines, burdens, problems, and disappointments. Life can be so complicated and so demanding these days. The truth is that we all need encouragement from time to time. We need someone to say "I love you" and "I believe in you." The word *encourage* literally means "to put the heart in," and the word *discourage* means "to tear the heart out." The good news of our Christian faith is that our Lord is a God of encouragement. When the world threatens to rip our hearts out, God is there for us with grace to encourage us, to put the heart back into us, to relight the spark, to give us new life.

At a recent meeting in Houston, I had dinner with a minister friend of mine. I asked him how he felt God's call to the ministry. His answer impressed me greatly. He said, "I owe so much to the church. It literally saved my life over and over." Then he continued:

"When I was a little boy growing up, my dad worked in the oil patch, so we had to move a lot. In fact, we moved so much that I went to eleven different schools in twelve years. It was really hard at first, all that moving, but I learned something pretty quickly that enabled me (even as a little kid) to handle all those changes and all those pressures. I knew that wherever we went, there would be a Sunday school teacher in a Methodist church just waiting to welcome me with open arms. The love and encouragement the church gave me held me up and kept me going, and eventually led me into the ministry."

I was so touched by that thought. He was saying, "Through the church and through a number of Sunday school teachers, I had tasted the encouraging love of God." As we talked there in that little restaurant, the food we were eating suddenly began to taste different. Actually, we were having the hamburger special, but all of a sudden it tasted like Holy Communion as we talked about the power of God's encouraging love.

Well, how is it with you right now? Have you tasted God's redeeming love? Have you tasted God's forgiving love? Have you tasted God's encouraging love? The word of the psalmist long ago is the word for you and me today: "O taste and see that the Lord is good."

NUMBER 7

Remember That

IT MATTERS INTENSELY WHAT YOU BELIEVE

Scripture: Matthew 17:1-8

t was business as usual in the San Diego County Sheriff's Office on that March afternoon in 1997. But then something happened to change all of that. The sheriff's deputy, Robert Brunk, was guiding his cruiser up the winding, hilly roads to Rancho Santa Fe, twenty miles north of San Diego. A couple of calls had come into the sheriff's office asking deputies to please check on relatives and friends at 18241 Colina Norte in Rancho Santa Fe.

When Deputy Robert Brunk got to the back door of the estate, he knew immediately that something was terribly wrong; there was a sickly odor coming from the house. He knew it was the smell of death, but he had no idea what awaited him inside. He entered the house and was shocked to see dead bodies everywhere. He counted up to ten bodies but had to go back outside for fresh air and to call for backup. Help quickly came from the sheriff's office and the coroner's office. Eventually they counted thirty-nine bodies inside the mansion.

The next day the police announced the cause of the deaths—a mixture of drugs and alcohol and suffocation. This mass suicide had happened in stages: Fifteen had died first (helped by others), then another fifteen, then seven, then the last two. Cult members lay on neatly made bunks in the seven bedrooms and throughout the house. All the members were dressed in comfortable black garb, including pleated collarless tunics and brand-new black-and-white athletic shoes. They wore black plastic wristwatches, and wide gold bands on their left ring fingers. Near each body was a neatly packed suitcase. Next to some were folded eyeglasses. Oddly, each person had a five-dollar bill and a bunch of quarters in his or her shirt pocket. Each had closely shorn hair. Some had pocketed the recipe for their death mixtures.

Purple death shrouds were draped over all but the last two members who died. They all wore arm patches with the words *Heaven's Gate* stitched at the top and *Away Team* along the bottom. There were no signs of struggle. Twenty-one women and eighteen men had organized and executed the mass suicide, leaving behind numerous videotapes, written tracts, and postings on the Internet in which they described their joy in escaping this life to move on to what they called "the Next Level."

Heaven's Gate cult leader Marshall Applewhite had convinced them that they were aliens who had been planted here years ago by a UFO, that another UFO was using the Hale-Bopp Comet as a shield, and that this spacecraft from the "Level Above Human" was coming to take them to their new world (paraphrase of S. J. Hedges, "www.masssuicide.com," *U.S. News & World Report*, April 7, 1997).

That much of the Heaven's Gate mystery was solved by good scientific and detective work, but so many questions haunt us: Why would a thirty-nine-year-old mother of five from Cincinnati leave everything, including two-week-old twins, to follow the teachings of Marshall Applewhite? Why would a seventy-two-year-old grandmother leave her home in Iowa to follow the cult? Why would all these people be so amazingly committed to this eerie sci-fi approach to religion that mixes computers and gnosticism, UFOs and mysticism, New Age and asceticism, mind-control and escapism? Why would they be so committed to this bizarre cult that they would willingly, indeed almost joyfully, participate in this mass suicide?

When I heard those first news reports about the deaths of cult leader Marshall Applewhite and his Heaven's Gate followers, my mind immediately flashed back to David Koresh and the Waco tragedy of April 1993. Then my mind went further back to November 1978, when Jim Jones and his followers drank cyanide-laced punch in Jonestown, Guyana; nine hundred and thirteen people died as they activated Jones' mass suicide plan.

Then I remembered a conversation I had a few weeks ago with a twelfth-grade student in one of our Houston high schools. He asked me, "Is religion always good?" I had to say to him, "No, religion is *not* always good. Some of the worst things that have ever happened in human history, people did because of their religion.

"Some people think that it doesn't really matter what you believe as long as you believe something. But it does matter. It does matter; it matters more than I can tell you.

"History has shown dramatically that wrongly motivated, mixed-up religion can be very bad and very destructive. Good religion is beautiful, creative, and constructive, and it enables people to do godlike things. Bad religion, on the other hand, is disastrous, and it produces fanatics who are narrow and negative, closed-minded, and sometimes even cruel."

The Crusades, the Inquisition, the Salem witch hunts, the crucifixion of Jesus, bloody wars, cruel persecution, brutal rituals, human sacrifices, strange superstitions, misdirected cults—they all have happened historically under the cloak of religion.

The point is clear: Religion can be very good, but when misdirected, it can be very bad. When religious ideas are high and true, they save, they heal, they make whole, they give new life. When they are low and false and all mixed up, they crush, they destroy, they devastate.

In the ancient marketplace, they had an interesting motto: Let the Buyer Beware! In other words, watch out; be cautious; don't be gullible; because you may be sold something that you really didn't want, and for an outrageous price.

It seems to me that that's a pretty good motto for the religious marketplace of our time. Believe me, there are lots of confusing religious ideas and appeals in our world today, all vying for your attention, all trying to win you to their way of thinking; so, it's a good idea to be very cautious. Let the buyer beware.

I also believe that it's a good idea to stay close to the mainline churches, those churches that are history-tested, time-honored, and trustworthy. Beware of the fly-by-night religious personality who zips into town with an easy 1-2-3-step program to salvation and a few exotic gimmicks, and then just as quickly zips away, never to be seen again. Beware of those who try to steal you away from your church by using smooth talk and fake smiles, and by suggesting ever so slyly that the church you are now in just isn't quite as spiritual as they are. Let the buyer beware.

Now, to help you find your way in the religious marketplace, let me give you a trustworthy shopping list. Let me show you the difference between a cult and a healthy faith by underscoring the best qualities of a creative, healthy faith.

Healthy Faith Keeps On Growing and Is Open
to New Truths from God

Cult leaders try to close the book on truth. They say, "Don't think, I will think for you. I will tell you what to do, what to believe, what to feel, and any-

50

one who questions me will be disciplined severely." Don't you see how wrong this is?

A call to Christian discipleship is a call to grow in the faith, to think, to stretch, to wonder, to probe, to love God with our minds. For this reason, we need to beware of any religion that shuts down thinking; we need to beware of any religion that says, "Here's what to believe. Accept this, and don't ask any questions; and don't bring any new ideas."

We also need to beware of being content with just one dramatic religious experience. This was Simon Peter's temptation during the Transfiguration. There he experienced Jesus, Moses, and Elijah. It was wonderful, powerful, mind-boggling. He knew God was in that place, and he wanted to stay there on that mountaintop. Jesus said to him, "Peter, this has been good, but we can't stay here. We must move on. We must be open to new experiences with God at other times and in other places."

Healthy faith keeps moving on and learning. Someone once said that religion is like a parachute; it works best when open. Healthy faith keeps stretching, ever open to new truth from God, while cults want to close the book on truth and shut down thinking. So, that's number one: Healthy faith keeps on growing.

51

Healthy Faith Works Now in Practical Daily Living

Underscore the word *now*. It gives us confidence for living *now*; it makes us better people *now*. Good religion is not just an insurance policy for another day, and not just an escape hatch to get us out of this world. Jesus came off the Mount of Transfiguration, and look at what he did: He went right down into the valley and healed an epileptic boy. This means that healthy faith is not just something that dwells in the past or longs for the future, but it works now, speaks to us now, makes us whole now.

Bishop Arthur Moore loved to tell the story of the man in Georgia who had been away from his hometown for some twelve years. The man had been involved in all kinds of shady practices and criminal activities. He had served several terms in jail. But when he came back home, he went to church; and when testimony time came, he was ready. He stood tall and said, "I'm so glad to be back home, and I want to tell you that while it's true that I have deserted my wife, forsaken my children, embarrassed my parents, stolen, lied, cheated, and done all manner of evil, and that I have served several terms in jail; I want you to know, my brothers and sisters, that not once in all that time did I ever lose my religion."

If your religion is nothing more than an insurance policy for heaven, if it has no effect on how you live *now* and how you treat others *now*, then you are missing out on life, and you'd better check out your motivation. Christianity is healthy faith because it encourages us to keep on growing, learning, and thinking, and because it works in practical daily living.

Healthy Faith Makes You More Loving

It inspires us to reach out in compassion and in service to others. On the other hand, many of the cults teach their followers the opposite—that everybody outside of our group is the enemy. But look what Jesus said about this. For him, love was the real measuring stick for healthy faith. In the Bible, the words are often used interchangeably: walk in faith, walk in love; put on faith, put on love. In the Bible, love is underscored over and over as the most genuine and reliable sign of mature discipleship.

Remember how Jesus put it: "A new commandment I give to you, that you love one another; as I have loved you. . . . By this all will know that you are My disciples . . ." (John 13:34-35 NKJV). And remember how the songwriter expressed it later: "They will know we are Christians by our love, by our love."

Remember how dramatically the apostle Paul put it: What does it matter if you can speak in tongues? If you don't have love, it's not worth anything. And what does it matter if you can do miraculous things? Without love, it's all empty and worthless. And what does it matter if you can spout high-sounding theology into the air? Without love, it's only so much noise. Faith, hope, love abide. These are the things that endure—these three: faith, hope, and love. But the greatest of these is love. So put love first; make love your aim. That's what God wants you to do (see 1 Corinthians 13).

If you have a religious experience, and it makes you more loving, then it is likely a valid experience; it is healthy faith. But if you have a religious experience that makes you narrow, hateful, judgmental, or "holier than thou," then I believe that is bad news and bad religion. Healthy faith asks, "What can I do for God and for others?" Unhealthy faith asks, "What's in it for me?" If you want to test your faith, one good way to do it is to just raise this question (the one Jesus emphasized): "Does my faith make me more loving?" Healthy faith keeps on growing, works in practical daily living, and makes us more loving.

Healthy Faith Puts Worship and Service Together

This is one of the greatest things that can be said about our Christian faith: It combines devotional life with spiritual action. We see this displayed dramatically in the Scripture lesson for this chapter, Matthew 17:1-8. Beautifully outlined in the Transfiguration story are three different approaches to religion.

First, there are the *pietists* (symbolized here by Simon Peter), who say, "Let's stay up here on the mountain; let's just worship here and not get smudged by the problems of the world."

Second, there are the *social activists* (symbolized here by the other disciples), who are down in the valley trying to heal, but can't do it because they have no power. They have no power because they haven't been up on the mountain.

Third, there is the *approach of Jesus*. He combines the two. He puts worship and service together. He puts devotion and social action together. He goes up on the mountain to worship, and then goes down into the valley to heal. Now, that's good, healthy religion.

Let me conclude with this: If you ever feel confused or perplexed by all the varied kinds of religions clamoring for your attention and allegiance; if you ever feel bewildered and wonder what is the difference between a cult and a healthy faith; then at that moment just bring your thoughts back home to Christianity's unique fact: Jesus of Nazareth. He is our pattern, our blueprint, our measuring stick, our Savior. He is the real test of genuine healthy faith.

The poet put it like this:

> Our Lord and Master of us all!
> Whate'er our name or sign,
> We own Thy sway, we hear Thy call,
> We test our lives by Thine.
>
> We faintly hear, We dimly see,
> In differing phrase we pray;
> But, dim or clear, we own in Thee
> The Light, the Truth, the Way!
>
> (John G. Whittier, "Our Master")

Number 6

Remember That

God Is Smarter Than You Are

Scripture: Luke 22:39-46

n the spring of 1995, our speaker for the Shamblin Lectures was my good friend John Claypool, who spoke to us (as only he can) about Christian hope. In that lecture series, Dr. Claypool said many meaningful and helpful things, but one of the most memorable moments was his retelling of an old, old story that came out of Chinese culture.

An elderly Chinese peasant farmer had a horse that he loved very much and depended on for almost everything. In the spring when it was time to plant, the farmer would hitch a plow to the horse and break the land. When the fall harvest would come in, the farmer would hitch the horse to a wagon and take his produce to the market to sell. Whenever the farmer had a distance to travel, he would put a saddle on the horse and ride it. Every day, in one way or another, this beloved horse was a big and dramatic part of the farmer's life.

Then one afternoon a bee stung the horse on its neck; the horse went into a panic and ran away. The farmer ran after the horse as it ran off into the hills, but, of course, the farmer couldn't catch up with the frightened animal. So at sunset, the farmer had to trudge back home and tell his wife that his beloved horse had run away.

Now, they lived in a small provincial village; and so, quickly the word spread that the farmer had lost his horse. For the next several days, whenever the farmer met any of his neighbors, they would say, "Sure sorry to hear about your bad luck in losing your horse," and he would just shrug his shoulders and say, "Bad luck, good luck; who's to say?"

Well, lo and behold, six days later his horse returned from the mountains with five wild horses that it had met. The farmer was able to corral all six of the horses and, of course, word spread quickly throughout the village. For the next several days, whenever he met anybody, they would say, "Sure glad to hear about your good luck getting all those horses." The farmer would just shrug his shoulders and respond, "Good luck, bad luck; who's to say?"

The farmer's son was excited about their new horses. He quickly began to try to break them so that his family could sell them for a big profit. But one of the horses bucked him off, and the son's leg was broken in three places. Word spread through the little village; and so for the next several days, whenever the farmer would meet his neighbors, they would say, "Sure sorry to hear about your bad luck, your boy getting hurt." Again, the farmer would just shrug his shoulders and respond, "Bad luck, good luck; who's to say?"

Two weeks later, a war broke out between the city states of interior China. The army came through conscripting every able-bodied male under the age of fifty to go and fight, and, of course, the farmer's son would have been in that category had the accident not happened. Because he had a broken leg, he didn't have to go, and that turned out to be very fortuitous because every villager who was conscripted wound up being killed in the war. And the old farmer said, "Good luck, bad luck; who's to say?"

I think the reason my friend John likes that story so much is because it reminds us that there are so many things we do not know. There are so many times in life when God can take something that seems so bad and, by the miracle of God's grace, turn it into something good. The story reminds us that sometimes what looks like our worst day can turn out to be our best day.

Nell Mohney wrote a book about this a few years ago. The title says it all: *Don't Put a Period Where God Put a Comma* (Nashville: Dimensions for Living, 1993). This is the message of Holy Week. The arrest of Jesus was not the end. The trial of Jesus was not the end. The crucifixion of Jesus was not the end. The burial of Jesus was not the end.

"There, that takes care of that," the world said. "We silenced him. We showed him. We stopped him," the world said. "So put a period there."

But God said, "No, that's not a period. It's just a comma, just a little ol' comma. It's not over. I've got a surprise for you. I've got a resurrection for you. It's not over, I've only just begun."

That's why we come to God in the spirit of humility and surrender, saying, "Thy will, O God, be done," because God knows what we cannot know and sees what we cannot see. Someone once said that we are like a fly crawling across an oil painting. We are so close to it, we can't see the big picture. God can, and so the best prayer is, "Thy will, O God, be done."

If you were asked to write down the two most famous prayers Jesus prayed, what would you write? Probably "The Lord's Prayer" and his prayer in the Garden of Gethsemane. But have you thought about this: The key theme of both of those prayers is "Father, thy will be done." Now let me bring this closer to home and underscore what that means for our lives today.

Praying "Thy Will Be Done" Means Coming to God in the Spirit of Trust

Jesus trusted God, and so can we.

Some years ago I had the unique privilege of working with D. L. Dykes. For twelve years I worked with him, and I learned more from D. L. in the first six months I worked with him than from all of my ministerial education courses put together. Whoever first came up with the phrase "legend in his own time" must have had D. L. or someone like him in mind. D. L. was indeed a legend. I could spend days telling "D. L. stories," but there is one in particular that taught me the meaning of coming to God in perfect trust.

Our staff had come up with a bold new program that we were so excited about and committed to. We were certain it would be a great thing to do, but it was going to take a lot of time, effort, energy, and resources. We had to convince the church's administrative board to approve the program and to give us the financial resources to do it right.

Finally, the night came to present the program to the board. We younger ministers on the staff were "pumped up" and ready to "wow the board" with our presentation.

"Why don't we go up to the sanctuary, kneel at the altar together, and pray before we go over to the board meeting?" D. L. said to us.

"Great idea," we thought.

The four of us went to the altar, knelt, and took turns praying. The three of us younger ministers prayed like this: "Lord, give us the right words to say in the right spirit. Give us the power of persuasion. Help us to convince the board to approve this. Help us show them how important this is. Open their hearts, Lord, and let them be receptive. . . ."

On and on we prayed. When we got through, very quietly and very humbly, D. L. began to pray. It was twenty years ago, and I still remember his exact words: "Father, if this is your will, bless us with success. If it is not your will, bless us with failure."

At first I wanted to grab him and say, "Oh, D. L.,

don't say that," but then as I thought about it, I realized that he was right. If it's not God's will, failure is a blessing; it's best not to succeed at it. If it's not God's will, it's best to not do it. That's what it means to pray "thy will be done," to pray in the spirit of complete trust. Prayer is not some arrogant attempt to tell God what God ought to do, or to convince God to do what we want God to do. Prayer is coming to God in trust and humility, saying, "Oh God, you know what is best. Show me how to get in line with that. Show me how to give my energy to that. Make me the instrument of your will."

Jesus was a person of prayer. All through the Gospels we see him praying. Therefore, we are not surprised here when he falls on his knees in the Garden of Gethsemane. It was the most natural thing in the world for him to do. This was a tough moment. The cross loomed before him. He prayed about this. Luke 22 puts it dramatically: "His sweat became like great drops of blood" (v. 44). That means this was serious business. He prayed about it in the spirit of trust; and in that intense experience, he found the strength to keep on trusting God and to say, "Not my will but [thy will be done]."

Praying "thy will be done" means coming to God in the spirit of trust.

Praying "Thy Will Be Done" Means Coming to God
in the Spirit of Obedience

Jesus was so obedient to the will of God. So
should we be.

Not too long ago a good friend of mine called
and told me to go to the fax machine because he
was going to fax me a prayer. I went. Here's what
he faxed: It was a contemporary prayer in which
a man is bragging to God about how well he has
done so far today. He asserts that he hasn't gos-
siped or lost his temper. He goes on to proudly
proclaim that he "hasn't been greedy or grumpy
or nasty or selfish so far today." But then comes
the punch line where he indicates that in just a
few minutes he will get out of bed and from that
point on he is going to need a lot of help from the
Lord!

That prayer in a tongue-in-cheek way reminds
us of how much we need help with our Christian
obedience. Christian obedience means applying
God's will to every situation, and seeing every
moment, every occurrence, every challenge,
every occasion as a unique opportunity to serve
God and to emulate the mind of Christ. But how
do we take on the mind of Christ? How do we
learn how to live every day in the spirit of Christian obedience?

Bud Wilkinson was without question one of the greatest football coaches of all time. He led his Oklahoma Sooners to several national championships. During the football season, Coach Wilkinson did an interesting thing: He had his quarterback move into his house and live with his family. Coach Wilkinson must have had an understanding wife!

Coach Wilkinson and the quarterback became like father and son. They lived under the same roof, they ate together, they rode to practice together, they studied films together, they diagrammed plays together, they discussed football constantly. Someone asked Coach Wilkinson why he did this. He answered, "Because if that young man spends enough time with me, he will begin to think like I think. And then when he gets out there on the football field, he will know what I want him to do."

That's what it means to be a Christian, to spend so much time with God that we begin to think like God thinks; and then when we get out there in the game of life, we will have the mind of Christ and know what he wants us to do. That's what Christian obedience means, to condition, train, and prepare ourselves to obey God in every circumstance and to apply God's will to every situation.

To pray "thy will be done" means to come to God in the spirit of trust and in the spirit of obedience.

Praying "Thy Will Be Done" Means Coming to God
in the Spirit of Commitment

Jesus was so committed to doing God's will. That's our calling, too.

I heard a story about a young man who walked into a card shop looking for an appropriate card for his girlfriend to express his undying love. The sales clerk showed him their best-selling card. It said simply, "To the only girl I have ever loved." The young man said, "That's terrific! I'll take six of those." Obviously that young man had trouble with commitment. Sometimes you and I do, too.

I once read an article about the training of Arabian stallions. Day after day, hour after hour, the stallions are taught to obey the master, to trust him completely, and to always respond promptly to his call. The master has a whistle, and when he sounds the whistle, the stallions are trained to stop, no matter what the circumstances, and come immediately to the master. Then as a final test, the stallions are placed in a corral in the desert, midway up a hill. At the bottom of the hill is a beautiful oasis with crystal blue waters.

The stallions stay in the corral for several hours under the blazing desert sun until they are frantic for water. Then the master stands at the top of the hill and the stallions are released from the corral.

Of course they all head straight for the water. But just before they reach it, the master blows the whistle. The horses who ignore the master's call and go on toward the water are considered not ready and must have further training. But the stallions who turn and go immediately to the master are considered well-trained, and they graduate. They are so totally committed to the master that they put his will before their own.

Are you that committed to God? That's what we see in Jesus, total trust, total obedience, and total commitment to the will of God. That's what it means to pray "thy will be done," to come to God in the spirit of trust, in the spirit of obedience, and in the spirit of commitment.

NUMBER 5

Remember That

EVERY NOW AND THEN WE ALL HEAR A ROOSTER CROW

Scripture: Mark 14:65-72

ot long ago I heard one of the most powerful men in Hollywood give a speech on the art of moviemaking. When he was asked about the increasing violence and obscenity in so many of today's films, he shouted an expletive and then said, "We have no moral responsibility at all. That's not our job. Our job is to make movies that make money. If violence and obscenity and depravity attract audiences, then so be it. That's exactly what we are going to give them."

When he said that, if you listened very carefully, you could hear somewhere way off in the distance the sound of a rooster crowing.

A TV news executive was asked recently about the graphic and numerous depictions of violence on the six o'clock news. He spewed out an expletive and then said, "Look, here's the rule: If it bleeds, it leads. Graphic violence attracts audiences, and audiences bring ratings, and ratings produce advertisers, and advertising puts money in my pockets. That's just the way it works."

As he said that, if you listened real carefully, you could hear somewhere way off in the distance the sound of a rooster crowing.

Some months ago, a big-name sports superstar was asked about his responsibility as a role model for the kids who admire and emulate him. He shouted out a four-letter word and then he said, "I'm no role model. That's the parents' job, not mine. Scoring points, winning games, getting endorsements—that's my job. If you don't like that, then that's your problem, not mine."

When he said that, if you listened real carefully, you could hear somewhere way off in the distance the sound of a rooster crowing.

One day I was with a group of people when suddenly they began to gossip. They were spreading ugly rumors about a friend of mine, crucifying my friend with vicious words. I started to say something, wanted to say something to defend my friend, but I didn't know those people very well, so I held my silence.

Later, as I walked to my car, I was kicking myself. I was feeling sad and ashamed that I hadn't seized the opportunity to stand tall and speak up.

"Why didn't I speak up?"

"Why didn't I do something to turn the conversation?"

"Why didn't I say a good word for my friend?"

Then I heard it. The unmistakable sound of a rooster crowing way off in the distance.

Have you ever had that experience? Have you ever failed like that? Have you ever missed your moment or shortcut your best self? Have you ever denied your faith? Have you ever heard a rooster crow?

Of course this all relates to that painstaking moment in Mark 14 in which Simon Peter denied his Lord three times. Earlier that night, Jesus and the disciples had gone to the Upper Room to share the Last Supper. Jesus told them that he would be betrayed by one of them and arrested, and that they would all fall away.

In typical fashion, Simon Peter boldly protested, saying, "Not me, Lord. I will not waver. Even if all the others fall away, I will not" (v. 29 paraphrased).

Then Jesus said to him, "[Simon], before the cock crows twice, you will deny me three times" (v. 30).

And that is exactly what happened. After Jesus was arrested, he was taken to the home of the high priest. Simon Peter followed and mingled with the servants in the courtyard. He was recognized as one of Jesus' disciples, but he denied it three times. Immediately he heard that sound of a rooster crowing. Peter broke down and wept.

Notice something here: The third time Peter denied his Lord, he began to curse and swear. It's interesting to note that after he cursed, they did not ask him again if he were a disciple.

The point is clear: Profanity and discipleship just don't go together. There are many marks of Christian faith and discipleship; profanity is not one of them.

Now, profanity is more than expletives. The problem is much deeper than that. Profanity is treating holy things, or human beings, or sacred relationships with contempt, disrespect, and disregard. Our words can be profane, but more than that, we can be profane in our attitudes and actions; none of that portrays discipleship.

Now, let me bring this closer to home. Let me underscore some of the ways we deny our Lord by being profane. Let's start with the most obvious.

Our Words Can Be Profane

Have you ever wondered why people swear? I asked several people whose opinions I respect, and I got a variety of answers.

1. Some said that people curse because they don't know any better. When I was a child, my parents used to say that to me, that it's a sign of ignorance and people who curse may need a dictionary as much as they need a Bible. They need to learn appropriate words to express themselves.

Well, that's one answer.

2. Others said that people use profanity because of a basic insecurity. The Scriptures tell us that a simple "yes" or "no" is sufficient. Yet some people feel so insecure within themselves and with their words that they find it necessary to color what they say with profanity in order to give it a ring of authority. They say, "They won't believe me and what I say unless I punch it up with dramatic expletives." Of course that is a sign of insecurity.

3. Some people use profanity because they are angry. They are seething inside, and every now and then that anger bubbles up in the form of profane language.

4. Another reason people use profanity is the mistaken notion that it brings acceptance. They think this is the way to be "one of the guys or gals," that cursing will show how "with it" and how grown-up they are; but really it only shows how immature they are.

5. Some people use profanity because they are insensitive, particularly to people around them.

Some months ago we had a local controversy about whether or not it should be legal to use profane language in a public place. Now, I don't know if it should be illegal or not, but I do know that it is insensitive.

6. Of course some people use profane words to "let off steam." Bishop Bob Goodrich once said that there are occasions when we need stronger words than we normally use. He used the examples of traffic jams, and lightbulbs that keep burning out.

Bishop Robert Goodrich said, "I favor the creation of a commission that could draw up a list of words approved for use by persons (including preachers) under circumstances of extreme provocation." He said that he tried *fiddle-faddle* and *twiddle-dee-dee*, but they were not adequate. He went on to say that strong language, though sometimes necessary, does not have to be vulgar, nor can any situation ever justify using the name of God in a curse.

After Simon Peter cursed, they did not ask him again if he were a disciple. Our words can be profane.

Our Attitudes Can Be Profane

Bishop Goodrich put it like this:

If you were to ask me to list the ten most profane persons I know, I would include three men who have

74

never used a dirty word, to my knowledge. I would include two who can lead a so-called good prayer in public. . . . All ten of them are members of some church. And yet, these would be included in the most profane people I know. Profanity, you see, is a many-sided thing, and some of its varieties have nothing to do with four-letter words. It's quite possible to be pious in language, proper in words, and profane in attitudes. (*Look at the Burning Bushes* [Atlanta: Spiritual Life Publishers], 1963)

What is that writer talking about? Simply this: Prejudice is profane. Hate is profane. Arrogance is profane. Disrespect is profane. So are jealousy, pettiness, resentment, bitterness, and ingratitude. Any attitude that hurts people or dehumanizes or depersonalizes is profane. Any attitude that treats persons or groups of people with contempt or disrespect is profane.

A few years ago I read a newspaper article about the shocking results of a survey of some seventeen hundred young people in Providence, Rhode Island. An unbelievable percentage of the sixth- to ninth-graders said in the survey that they thought it was okay for a man to force himself on a woman if he had spent money on her, or if they had been dating for six months.

You see, that kind of attitude is profane because it endorses the abuse of another person. To use or abuse another person in any way is wrong. Our words can be profane, and our attitudes can be profane.

Our Actions Can Be Profane

To underscore this, here is a true story that is a little graphic. But we need a strong illustration to make a strong point.

It happened a few years ago on a beach in Florida. The college students had gone to Fort Lauderdale, as they do every year, to celebrate spring break. Larry, a campus minister friend of mine, goes there each year to help with worship services on the beach and with counseling, and to be a peacemaker and an influence for good. He goes there to quietly witness for the Christian faith.

One year Larry saw a young freshman student from Michigan who was wearing a T-shirt that had on the front of it, "Help Stamp Out Virginity!" That T-shirt bothered Larry, so he began to look for an opportunity to talk with the young man about it.

Finally, one morning while walking on the beach, Larry bumped into the student. He had on that T-shirt again. They walked together for awhile, enjoying the sights and sounds of the morning surf, and even looking for seashells.

Suddenly Larry said, "I like your T-shirt."

The student beamed and said, "Thanks."

Then Larry said, "In fact, I like your T-shirt so much that I want to make a suggestion. When you get back home, I want you to take that T-shirt off very carefully, fold it neatly, put it in a sturdy box, wrap it with tissue paper, put some mothballs in there, and put it away in a safe place. And some years from now, when you are married, and when that first young man comes over to take your daughter out on her first date, I want you to give him that T-shirt."

The student looked at Larry angrily, said nothing, then turned and ran off down the beach.

Larry thought at first that he had gone too far. But later that day he saw the young man again; this time the student was wearing a sweatshirt that had the words *Michigan State* on it.

He walked over to Larry and said, "Mister, I don't know who you are, but I want you to know that I burned that T-shirt. I guess I really hadn't thought that through."

Our words can be profane. Our attitudes can be profane. Our actions can be profane. But there is one thing we need to remember: After Simon Peter cursed, they never asked him again if he were a disciple. Every time we express profanity in words or attitudes or actions, we are denying our Lord. Profanity and discipleship: They just don't go together.

NUMBER 4

Remember That

YOU DON'T HAVE TO CROSS THE FOX RIVER UNTIL YOU GET TO IT

Scripture: Matthew 14:22-33

 n the early days of the settling of America, Thomas Jefferson and a group of men were traveling cross-country on horseback when they stopped at a wayside inn one night to rest. While the men were having dinner, one member of the group said, "Well, my friends, we face the most difficult part of our journey tomorrow. Tomorrow we have to cross the dangerous Fox River."

The Fox River was noted for its constantly changing nature. Some days it was deep. Some days it was shallow. Some days the water was fast and treacherous. Other days it was quiet and serene. Some days there was a strong undertow; some days there was not. Recognizing this, the men then discussed about how they should cross the Fox River the next day. Should they ride their horses across? Should they walk? Should they swim? Should they send scouts up and down the banks of the river, looking for the safest place to cross? Should they buy boats, or build rafts, or maybe even take the time to construct a makeshift bridge? How should they do it? What would be the best way for them to safely cross the dangerous Fox River?

On and on the men went, discussing all the different ways they might get across the river. The more they talked, the more alarmed and anguished they became. Then, the door of the inn opened, and in came Trapper William, the most noted scout and outdoorsman of that area. The men in Thomas Jefferson's party were thrilled to see Trapper William because they knew that he knew the region so well. He had crossed the Fox River many, many times.

They called him over to their table and asked him for advice.

"Trapper William, it's good to see you. We want to ask you this: What's the best way to cross the Fox River? Should we ride across on our horses, or swim, or walk, or build a raft or a bridge? What have you found in your experience to be the best way to get across?"

Trapper William sensed their fears. He could hear the anxiety in their voices, and quietly he said to them, "I have crossed the Fox River many times in many different ways over the years. Because the river is always changing, it can be precarious, so I have only one rule with regard to crossing the Fox River: I never cross it until I get to it."

Trapper William's rule for the Fox River is also a pretty good guideline for life: "Don't cross it until you get to it." In other words, Don't let your fears undo you. Don't work yourself into a fretful frenzy. Don't borrow trouble. Take life as it comes—one day at a time, one step at a time, one challenge at a time—knowing as a Christian that God will be with you and will see you through. Too many of us, however, have a way of inventing fears, magnifying problems, and exaggerating potential threats. Research has shown that 92 percent of all our fears are never realized—92 percent of the things we fear and worry about never happen! This truth was emphasized in a recent *Peanuts* comic strip.

Charlie Brown is sitting in the nurse's office at school. In frame 1, he says, "So, here I am about to see the school nurse." In frame 2, he says, "She will probably just take my temperature and look at my throat." In the third frame, Charlie Brown's fears begin to take hold, and he says, "Maybe she'll take a blood sample. I hope she doesn't take a blood sample. Maybe she'll just weigh me, but then again maybe she'll want to give me a shot." By frame 4, Charlie Brown is in a panic and says: "If she even mentions exploratory surgery, I'll scream!"

The grip of fear can be most devastating. Fear can rob us of life. Elizabeth O'Connor, in her book *Cry Pain, Cry Hope* (Dallas: Word, 1987), puts it like this: "When I reflect deeply on my life and what I really want, it is not to be afraid. When I am afraid, I am miserable. I play it safe. I restrict myself. I hide [my] talent in the ground. I am not deeply alive, the depths of me are not being expressed. When I am afraid, a tiny part of me holds captive most of me. When I am afraid, I am a house divided against itself. So more than anything else, I want to be delivered from fear. . . ."

Who can deliver us from fear? Who can give us courage and strength and poise when the storms of life threaten us? Well, the answer is found here in Matthew 14. The disciples were caught in a frightening storm. Jesus went to them most dramatically in their time of need, and the first thing he said to them was, "Don't be afraid. Take heart.

I am here. Don't be afraid" (v. 27 paraphrased). He walked on the water—a graphic reminder to us that when we are in trouble, that's when Christ can come most miraculously and powerfully into our lives, if we are open to him.

Look at the words and phrases that Matthew uses to describe the plight of the disciples: "battered by the waves"; "the wind was against them"; "terrified"; "they cried out in fear." But then came Jesus, bringing peace, courage, confidence, and hope: "Take heart, it is I; I am here. Have no fear" (v. 27 paraphrased). Recently I ran across a remarkable statistic in which someone researched the Scriptures and found that the words "fear not" or "don't be afraid" are in the Bible—are you ready for this?—three hundred and sixty-five times! Think of that: That's one "fear not" for each day of the year.

Now, of course, we all know that some fears are helpful. We should be careful where we walk at night. We should be sensible and cautious about what we put into our bodies. We should be afraid of wild beasts, violent people, and drunk drivers. But that's not the kind of fear I'm talking about. I'm talking about the kind of destructive fear that undoes, paralyzes, and robs us of the abundant life that Jesus came to bring us. Let me be more specific. Let me stress three places where we don't have to be afraid anymore.

Don't Be Afraid to Trust God

When the storms of life come (as they will for all of us) don't be afraid to trust God. As a matter of fact, I have noticed that God is closest to us, and most powerfully with us, when we are hurting. Maybe it's partly because we are more open to God when we are down and out, but I also believe that God is like a loving parent, and loving parents want desperately to be with their children when their children are in pain.

"Precious Lord," one of the most popular gospel songs of all time, was written back in the 1930s by Thomas Dorsey. That song established him as one of the architects of gospel music. The appeal of the song crosses all denominational lines and has been translated into some thirty-two languages. During the 1920s, Dorsey had become famous as a jazz musician. He became intrigued with the thought of blending jazz and blues with church music.

In August of 1932, Dorsey was scheduled to be the featured soloist in a St. Louis church. His wife was expecting a baby at the time, and he was worried about leaving her at home in Chicago. Later he said, "Something was telling me to stay." But he decided to keep his commitment, and so he left for St. Louis. During his performance that night,

84

a Western Union telegram arrived. When he opened it, the telegram had four words that broke his heart and crushed his spirit: *Your wife just died.*

He quickly returned home to Chicago and learned that his wife had given birth to their first-born son just before she died. Later that night the baby died.

He buried Nettie and their son in the same casket. Then Dorsey fell apart. For days he closeted himself. He said he felt that God had done him an injustice. Dorsey didn't want to serve God anymore or write any more gospel songs.

But then one day he sat down at the piano. His hands began to browse the keys, he said, and then something happened.

He felt as though he could reach out and touch God. He found himself playing a melody he had never heard before, and suddenly words came into his head. They just seemed to fall in place.

> Precious Lord, take my hand,
> Lead me on, let me stand . . . .

Dorsey, in this beloved song, went on to reaffirm his faith in God, asking God to take him by the hand, hold him up, give him strength, and lead him through this difficult storm. Dorsey was absolutely convinced that the words and the melody came to him as a direct gift from God. He went on to write more than four hundred gospel songs, including "The Old Ship of Zion," "My Desire," and "There'll Be Peace in the Valley for Me."

Dorsey said he learned that when we are in our deepest grief, when we feel farthest from God, is when we are most open to that restoring power. And this is when God is most near. This is one of the greatest messages of the Bible: When the storms of life come, fear not. Don't be afraid to trust God.

Don't Be Afraid to Celebrate Life

Read these words I ran across not too long ago and see if you can figure who might have said them:

> Fear of failure, fear of success, fear of losing your health, fear of losing your mind.
> Fear of being taken too seriously, fear of not being taken seriously enough.
> Fear that you worry too much, fear that you don't worry enough.
> Your mother's fear that you'll never marry, your father's fear that you will.
> Fear of the unknown? Forget it. Fear of too many roads and not enough time? Maybe.
> But go ahead, put one foot in front of the other. And just do it.

Who said that? Billy Graham? Leo Buscaglia? Norman Vincent Peale? Mother Teresa? a statesman? a preacher? a psychiatrist? No, none of these. Actually the words are from a Nike commercial. The words have very little to do with athletic shoes. The writer of that ad knows that fear is real, that we are a fearful people, and that many people today are so fear-frozen that they forget to seize the moment and celebrate life.

This is one thing I love about Simon Peter here in Matthew 14 and throughout the Gospels. He is so full of life, so on the cutting edge. He is always ready to take the plunge. He wants to live life to the full. "Lord, I see you walking on the water. Let me try it, too. Let me taste the miracles of life" (v. 28 paraphrased).

Erma Bombeck wrote a best-seller a few years ago that was different from her other books of humor. It was entitled *I Want to Grow Hair, I Want to Grow Up, I Want to Go to Boise* (New York: HarperCollins, 1990). This book grew out of Bombeck's visit to Camp Sunrise in the mountains outside of Payson, Arizona—a camp designed for children who are battling cancer. The title comes from a child who shared his priorities with a camp leader: "My three wishes are (1) to grow hair; (2) to grow up; and (3) to go to Boise."

The book is a glowing testament of hope manifested in countless boys and girls who must grow up quickly as they cope with catastrophic illness, and who must learn quickly how to seize the moment and smell the roses daily. Bombeck said that at first she didn't think she would find much humor among the campers, but discovered, to her own spiritual growth, how close humor is to love, hope, and faith. As one teenager said to her, "Would you be happier if we cried all the time?"

The book vibrates with the exuberant lives of those who have faced and overcome their fears, and who are now daily kissing the joy while it flies. Let me quote one paragraph that says it all:

> Kids with cancer seem to have a gift for cutting through the "what ifs," "what should've beens," "what might have beens," and get directly to "what is now." Bert was five years old and fighting neuroblastoma. He loved to draw. One day when a visitor asked him, "Are you going to be an artist when you grow up?" Bert replied matter-of-factly, "I'm an artist now."

What are we waiting for? This too is one of the great themes of the Bible. Life is God's gift to us. Seize it, taste it, experience it, savor it, share it, and thank God for it. Don't be afraid to trust God, and don't be afraid to celebrate life.

Don't Be Afraid to Face Death

When that storm hit, the disciples were terrified. They were afraid they were going to die.

Then along came Jesus to calm the storm without and within—the storm on the sea and the one in their hearts. When he did that, they fell down before him and said, "Truly you are the Son of God."

We sometimes talk about being scared to death, and lots of people are scared of death, but as Christians we don't have to be. God will see us through even that storm called death.

Let me illustrate it this way: Sometime ago I had surgery. I wasn't fearful about that; I trusted my doctor completely. But I wasn't real crazy about being put to sleep. Now, let me tell you why. I can get claustrophobic, and the last time I had been put to sleep was when I was twelve years old. I had appendicitis and was rushed to the emergency room. I remember being on the stretcher and being rushed down the hallway into this big room with all these big lights. I remember all these big people standing over me and putting something on my face—ether, just smothering me. It was frightening for a little boy. I thought, "I don't want to go through that again." So I asked the anesthesiologist (who is my neighbor) about it; he just grinned and said, "Jim, we've come a long way since then."

When we got into the operating room, they began to talk about what size mallet they should use to hit me in the head with to knock me out. Then, finally, the doctor had an IV attached to me.

He said, "Jim, are you ready? I'm going to start the medication."

I said, "I'm ready."

In about four seconds, he said, "How do you feel? Do you feel any different?"

"Well, I just feel pleasant."

Then a nurse tapped me on the shoulder and said, "Jim, would you like a cup of ice?"

I said, "I'd love a cup of ice, but they told me not to have anything to eat or drink before the surgery."

She said, "Honey, you're in the Recovery Room."

It was over. It was done. I thought to myself, "You know, death for a Christian is probably like that. You come up to it having to trust those around you and the one above you, and then you just go to sleep. Then somewhere in heaven, somebody taps you on the shoulder and says, 'Would you like a cup of ice? Honey, you're in heaven.'"

Isn't that a beautiful thought? You know, we don't have to be afraid of death because God is on both sides of the grave. And nothing, not even death, can separate us from God.

Let me conclude with something I heard that touched me deeply:

When bedtime came for the little lad in our house, there was an unforgettable ritual he would invite us to share in. Coming to my chair, he would climb up on my lap. Turning his face to mine, with a look of simple trust, he would say in a tone brushed with sleepiness, "Daddy, walk my hand to bed."

And that is my constant prayer, as I try to make the most of my life. Dear God, please walk my hand to this task, through this sorrow, through this fear. And somewhere in the tomorrows, when the great sleep comes for me, I will remember my little boy's words and pray, "Dear God, walk my hand to bed." (From a sermon by Don Shelby, June 19, 1994)

Throughout the pages of the Bible, Jesus says to us over and over, Don't be afraid to trust God; don't be afraid to celebrate life; and don't be afraid to face death.

Remember That

THERE ARE SOME ROADS WE JUST DON'T NEED TO GO UP

Scripture: 1 Thessalonians 5:16-18

Some years ago, when I was starting out in the ministry, I was sent to serve a church way out in the country in Tennessee.

On the first Sunday I was there, after morning service, I was standing at the door of the church speaking to the people as they filed out. I was feeling pretty good; I thought things had gone pretty well.

But then the board chairman came by. He shook my hand and said, "Now, Jim, go ahead and greet the folks, but when you get through, come on back to the Sunday school classroom to the right of the pulpit. Four of us would like to visit with you back there in private for just a few minutes."

Oh no, I thought to myself, what did I do wrong?

Obviously he saw the concern on my face, and quickly he said, "Don't worry. You did great this morning. We're thrilled to have you here. We just want to ask a favor of you. It won't take long."

A few minutes later, when I arrived at the classroom, four of the top leaders of the church were standing there waiting for me.

"Now, Jim," they said, "We just want to ask you for a favor, and we want you to agree to do this and not ask any questions."

"Could you help me a little bit?" I asked.

"Sure," they said. "Have you noticed that, as you head south out of town, there's a little gravel road that goes off to the right?"

"Yes, I know where you're talking about. It's just beyond the Edwardses' house," I said.

That's right, they nodded. Then they said the strangest thing.

"The favor is this: Please don't go up that road for thirty days, and don't ask us why. It's for your own good, Jim. Just for thirty days, don't drive up that road. After thirty days, you can go anywhere you want to go."

I thought to myself, This is weird, the strangest request I've ever heard. But I played along.

"Do we have any church members who live up that road?"

"No," they said.

"Is there any reason why I might need to go up that road?"

"No."

Finally, I said, "I don't understand this at all, but if you're absolutely sure I won't need to go up there for any reason, I guess I could agree to that."

They seemed so relieved. They smiled and thanked me and patted me on the back. As I drove home from church, I was mystified by that strange conversation and that unusual request.

About a week later, I found out why they didn't want me to go up that gravel road—because the county sheriff went up there. By the way, the sheriff's name was Buford Pusser, and later a best-selling book was written and a popular movie was made about Sheriff Pusser's trip up that road.

The book and movie *Walking Tall* described dramatically how Sheriff Pusser went up that gravel road to shut down the moonshine stills that were in operation in the hilly backwoods of Tennessee.

When the news about Sheriff Pusser's raid on the moonshiners hit the media, the board chairman came to see me and said, "Now, Jim, you know why we didn't want you to go up that gravel road. You were new in town. We were afraid that if you went up that road the moonshiners might think you were a revenuer and shoot at you. We didn't want our new preacher to drift into a highly dangerous situation."

I asked, "What about the thirty days? What was that all about?"

He said, "Well, in thirty days everybody in the county will know you and your car; then if you drove up there, the moonshiners would recognize you and they would lie low, but they wouldn't shoot at you. We knew Sheriff Pusser was going to take care of this soon, but in the meantime, we were trying to protect you from a dangerous situation up that road."

Now, the way those men chose to handle that predicament is open to question, but their intention was good. They were trying (in their way) to save me from a very real danger.

That story is a graphic reminder that—sad as it is to say it—there are indeed roads in this life that are a real threat to our physical well-being. We all know this. "Whatever you do, don't go up that road." "Don't get off on that side street." "Don't go down that road at night." "Don't cut through that dark alley."

All of our lives we have heard those kinds of warnings about dangerous roads. Unfortunately, they are a part of life in this world. But have you thought about this: There are also dangerous roads spiritually?

That's why the apostle Paul wrote all of his letters, which now make up a big part of the New Testament—to warn the early churches about those dangerous roads.

Here in 1 Thessalonians, Paul is writing to the church at Thessalonica because he saw them drifting down dangerous roads spiritually. He saw that selfishness, pride, and ingratitude were threatening to tear that church apart. So, Paul wrote to straighten them out and to warn them about these dangerous roads. In essence, he was saying, "Don't be selfish, don't be prideful, and especially don't be so ungrateful." His message to them can be summed up in one verse: "Give thanks in all circumstances; for this is the will of God in Christ Jesus for you" (v. 18).

Just live every day, every moment, in the spirit of thanksgiving and you won't get off track. You won't wander down those dangerous roads. Gratitude: That's the road the Christian walks daily.

Now, let's bring this into sharper focus by coming in the back door and looking at these dangerous roads that the apostle Paul was so concerned about.

Don't Go Up the Dangerous Road of Selfishness

Selfishness is one of the most perilous roads I know of spiritually because it leads directly to greed and egotism and emptiness.

One morning a man went to see the pastor of an inner-city church. He told the pastor a terribly distressing story of poverty and misery in the neighborhood. "This poor widow," he said, "has four hungry children to feed. She's sick in bed, with no money for a doctor. And besides that, she owes three months' rent and is about to be evicted. If she doesn't come up with $600 today, she and her four children will be put out on the streets tonight. I wonder if you can help?"

The pastor was deeply touched. "I certainly can help," he said. "If you can give your time to this worthy cause, so can I. By the way, who are you? Are you a friend, or a member of the family?"

"Neither," said the man. "I'm the landlord."

Selfishness is not a pretty picture, is it?

There is another story about a woman who called the Butterball turkey company and said, "I've had a Butterball turkey in my freezer for twenty-three years; is it safe to eat it?"

The company representative said, "Has your freezer been on all the time?" "Oh yes," the woman answered.

"Well, then," said the representative, "it would be safe to eat, but it probably wouldn't taste too good."

"That's what I thought" said the woman, "so I'll just give it to the church."

Alfred Alder, the noted psychologist, once put an ad in the newspaper that read: "Guaranteed: Fourteen-Day Cure for Loneliness."

A woman showed up at his office, ad in hand, and said, "It says here that you can cure my loneliness in fourteen days. Is that true?"

"Absolutely," said Dr. Adler. "If you will do exactly what I tell you to do for fourteen days, you won't be lonely."

"Tell me more," said the woman.

Dr. Adler said, "For fourteen consecutive days, I want you to go out and do something kind for somebody else."

The woman said, "Why should *I* do something kind for somebody else?" To which Dr. Adler replied, "In your case, it might take twenty-one days."

When we go up that dangerous road of selfishness and resentment, we end up bitter and miserable and lonely. On the other hand, when we live each day in the spirit of thanksgiving to God, in the spirit of self-giving love to others, we find meaning and purpose and joy.

When Paul said, "Give thanks in all circumstances," at least a part of what he meant was this:

Don't give in to selfishness. Don't go up that dangerous road. That road is a threat to your soul.

Don't Go Up the Dangerous Road of Pride

Now, I know that there is a good kind of pride. We should be proud of our church and our children and our nation. But that's not what I'm talking about, and that's not what Paul was concerned about. Paul was concerned about the brand of pride that makes people arrogant and hypocritical, the kind that is the opposite of humility.

There was a man whose great ambition was to become a general in the Army. He imagined all the attention he would get—everybody saluting him, somebody to drive him around, all the perks of that high rank.

One day he reached his goal. He was promoted to brigadier general. He moved into his new office, sat behind his big desk, felt the power emanating from that office.

His aide walked in, saluted, and said, "Sir, there's a man here to see you."

The general said, "Send him right in."

The general began to swell with pride, thinking that he had arrived at this place on his own. He thought, "I'm going to impress this visitor with how important I am and how much power I have."

So, just as the visitor walked in, the general wheeled around, grabbed the phone, and pretended that he was talking to the president of the United States.

He said, "Mr. President, I understand your position on this. Just trust me, and I will handle that for you. I have a good idea about how to get that done, and I will share it with the Secretary of Defense when I see him tomorrow. Thank you for calling. Goodbye, Mr. President."

The general hung up the phone, turned around, and saw this ordinary soldier standing there. The general barked at him, "As you can see, Private, I'm a very busy man, but is there anything I can do for you?"

The soldier said, "Nothing, sir. I'm just here to hook up your phone."

Now, that's a light treatment of a very serious subject. Arrogant pride can be devastating to our souls. It robs us of our sense of humor. It makes us stuffy, pretentious, overbearing, hypocritical, and it destroys the spirit of gratitude within us because it dupes us into thinking we deserve all the credit.

If you go back and study the New Testament closely, you will discover that Jesus' strongest rebukes were directed toward arrogant and prideful people. Paul saw the danger, too, and he said:

Don't go up that dangerous road of selfishness, and don't go up that dangerous road of pride.

Don't Go Up the Dangerous Road of Ingratitude

Do you remember Bennett Cerf's classic story about a man named Joe, who one day came to see his friend named Sam?

"Sam, I'm in need of a little help. Could you lend me $2,000 until next Friday?"

"Absolutely not," said Sam, "No way."

"But Sam," Joe protested, "don't you remember how some years back, when your investments in the stock market failed, I was the one who gave you $10,000 to keep you from being wiped out?"

"Yes."

"And, don't you remember that when your daughter became critically ill, I was the one who took her to that clinic in Florida and paid for her care?"

"Yes."

"And, don't you remember just a few years ago when we were fishing together; you fell out of the boat, and I was the one who jumped into the rapids and saved you from drowning?"

"Yes."

"Well, then Sam, why in heaven's name won't

you lend me $2,000 for one week when I need it so desperately?"

Sam was quiet for a minute; then slowly he said, "All the things you say are true, Joe, but the big question is, What have you done for me lately?"

Ingratitude is not a pretty picture, is it? And yet, isn't that what we say to God? "Oh sure, God, you have given me life and family and friends and more blessings than I could ever count, but the big question is, What have you done for me lately?"

Put that over against this: I received a beautiful letter from a ninety-one-year-old woman who lives in Baytown, Texas. Let me share with you just a portion of her letter; it reads:

> Dear Jim,
>
> The reason I'm writing to you today is to express my appreciation to you and to all the good folks at your church. I love watching your worship service on television. I tune in every Sunday. Thank you for making it possible.
>
> I would like to explain why I am not in church on Sunday. I am ninety-one years old now, and I live out my days all alone in a wheelchair. I have served the Lord since I was sixteen. I [had] taught young people in Sunday school since I was twenty-one until just a few years ago when my leg was amputated and I was confined to this wheelchair.
>
> I can't go and teach and visit and help people anymore, so the way I serve God now is to write letters of

103

appreciation to people. So, let me say, "Thank you, and God bless you. God bless your family. And God bless St. Luke's."

P.S.: By the way, I pray for you twice each day.

Isn't that something? A ninety-one-year-old woman in a wheelchair writing letters of gratitude and reminding us that it's a beautiful thing to say thanks to other people and that it's a sacred thing to say thanks to God.

If the apostle Paul could speak to us today, we know what he would say, don't we? He would say: Don't go up the road of selfishness; don't go up the road of arrogant pride; and don't go up the road of ingratitude. Instead, "give thanks in all circumstances; for this is the will of God in Christ Jesus for you."

Number 2

Remember That

You Do Better When You Try

Scripture: Matthew 25:14-18

n a recent vacation, we went to church in Dallas with our son Jeff and his wife, Claire. We went to Christ United Methodist Church to hear our good friend Don Underwood preach.

Don did a great job preaching and leading the service. To top it all off, something happened at the end of the service that I had never seen happen. It was magnificent, one of those unique and unexpected moments that will stay with us for a long, long time.

When the invitation was given and the hymn of commitment was sung, three families came forward to join the church. They were received warmly and introduced to the congregation. Don asked them the loyalty question: "Will you be loyal to The United Methodist Church and uphold it with your prayers, your presence, your gifts, and your service?" Then Don told them the answer: "Your answer is 'I will.' "

All the adults answered dutifully and somewhat routinely, "I will." But one five-year-old boy with a burr haircut, who looked like mischief personified, shouted out as loud as he could, "I'll try!"

Don doubled over with laughter, the congregation applauded, and (as we were sitting down near the front) Don then turned to me and said, "Jim, I've been in the ministry for over twenty years, and that was probably the most honest answer to that question I have ever heard."

Wasn't that beautiful? With childlike innocence and honesty, that five-year-old boy said, "I'll try. I'll try my best."

You know, that's what God asks of us. God doesn't demand that we be perfect. God doesn't even demand that we be successful. God just calls us to be faithful. God calls us to try our best and then trust him to handle the rest.

Some months ago we had the memorial service in our sanctuary for one of our saints. Edith Park had lived life faithfully and zestfully for one hundred and three years, five months, and one day.

But Mrs. Park was remarkable not only because she lived actively for one hundred and three years, but even more because of the quality of her life, of her faith, hope, and love.

Over all those one hundred and three years, she never quit on life; she kept on trying her best. In her nineties, she went on a whirlwind trip around the world. In her nineties, she climbed the Great Wall of China, running ahead of her family; she was so excited and anxious to experience that— and to get to the top so that she could look over into Mongolia. In her nineties, she stood on the equator in Kenya, with one foot in one hemisphere and one foot in the other. In her nineties, she rode a camel in the desert in Egypt, and she duck-walked up a narrow passageway to the top of one of the Pyramids. (That's so difficult to do that they won't let folks try that anymore, but Edith Park did it.) And when she was over one hundred years old, she enrolled in an exercise class and refused to use the elevator in the building where she lived, choosing instead to walk up and down the stairs.

No question about it, she had great genes; but even more, she had a great positive faith and a great positive attitude. She refused to give up, she refused to give in, she kept on living and loving and learning. She never missed a Sunday at church. Unless she was out of town or sick in bed,

107

she was always here, sitting in her favorite pew, smiling radiantly, and blowing kisses to everybody. A long time ago she made a commitment to Christ and his church, a commitment in which she said, "I'll try. Lord, I'll try my best."

Psychologists tell us that as long as we live, we have two desires working within us, doing battle against each other. One is the desire to give up, to pull back, to throw in the towel and quit on life. The other is the desire to keep on trying, to move forward through struggle and effort by stretching, growing, and celebrating life. Of course the call of the Christian is to move forward and embrace life. But, sadly, far too many people forget that, and they just fold up their tents. They feel that life is too hard, that life has dealt them a poor hand, a hand not nearly so favorable as others are holding, so they quit; they refuse to try anymore.

Jesus once told a parable about this kind of quiet tragedy. We call it the parable of the talents. A more contemporary name might be the parable of investments. Like all of his parables, this one is a simple story, and yet so profound in its implications and lessons. Remember the parable with me.

Once there was a well-to-do businessman who decided to take a trip. The man had three associates with whom he left his fortune. To one, he gave $50,000 in silver. To another, he gave

$20,000; and to still another, he gave $10,000. He instructed the men to work with the money, to use the money, to invest the money for an appropriate return and profit. Now, sometime later, when the businessman returned home from his travels, he called in his three associates for a report.

The first two men had invested their money and had done quite well; they were commended for a job well done. But the third man had been afraid to even try. He had done nothing but hide the money in the ground. His lack of imagination and lack of effort cost him dearly. Not only did he miss out on a promotion, but he lost all the money and his position as well.

Apathy, you see, is so costly. Not trying, quitting on life, is so sad. Jesus shows us that in this parable. He also exposes the perfect formula for failure. The one-talent servant failed because he didn't try for three reasons: First, he didn't appreciate what he had. Second, he didn't accept what he had; and third, he didn't use what he had. Let's take a look at these three ideas.

He Didn't Appreciate What He Had

Can't you just hear him complaining? "I didn't get as much as the others. It's not fair! How can I hope to compete with them? It's not right, so I

won't play the game. I'll show 'em. I won't participate at all."

The sounds of bitterness, apathy, and ingratitude. He got $10,000 before inflation, but he did-
n't appreciate it. In fact, he resented it because, in
his mind, what he had paled in comparison to the
others who had more.

J. Wallace Hamilton, in his book *Ride the Wild
Horses* (Nashville: Abingdon, 1980), tells a wonderful story about how easy it is to take for
granted what we have. It's about a farmer who
had lived on the same farm all his life and was
tired of it, bored with it. He had inherited the
farm from his parents, but now he was miserable
there and desperately craved a change. He sub-
jected everything on the farm to his own blind
and merciless criticism. At last, he decided to
sell the old place and buy another more to his
liking.

So, he listed the farm with a real estate agent,
who came out, looked over the property, and then
prepared a sales advertisement for the newspaper.
However, before giving the ad to the newspaper,
the agent read to the farmer the very flattering
description: "Beautiful, spacious farmhouse; ideal
location; excellent barn, good pasture, fertile soil,
up-to-date equipment, well-bred stock; near town,
near church; good neighbors."

"Wait a minute," said the farmer, "read that again, and take it slow."

Again, the description was read: "Beautiful, spacious farmhouse; ideal location. . . ."

"Changed my mind," said the farmer. "I'm not gonna sell. All my life, I've been looking for a place just like that."

Can't we relate to that? The farmer was living in a paradise and didn't know it.

Russell Conwell's great lecture, "Acres of Diamonds," which he gave more than six thousand times, was built around this idea. Dr. Conwell stressed that the riches of life are all around us wherever we are, but so often our eyes fail to see them for the simple reason that we magnify the difficulties, overlook the advantages, and fail to see the good in what we have. The one-talent servant in Jesus' parable had this problem, and often, too often, so do we. The servant failed because he didn't appreciate what he had.

He Didn't Accept What He Had

Jesus' parable reminds us that we can't always determine the size of our talents. That is, there are certain givens that we have to learn to live with, things that will not budge and cannot be altered. All the bitterness in the world would not have changed the fact that the man received one talent. That's what he was given; that's what he had to work with. No matter how much energy we expend, no matter how much we may wish it were otherwise, there are some things in life—in your life and mine—that will not change. Life has limits that we must learn to accept.

This is partly what the Adam and Eve story is about in the book of Genesis. God placed them in the garden and gave to them incredible possibilities. They could name the animals and subdue them. They could till the earth, they could enjoy all the wonderful works and blessings of nature, and they could feast on the fruit of the land. Indeed, Adam and Eve could do anything except one thing. They had one limitation: They were not to eat the fruit of one tree in the garden. It's almost as if this is a reminder that we are not God; we have some limits on our lives. There are some things we cannot do and some things we cannot change.

We must all come to terms with the "trees" in our lives: Those of us 5' 11" tall cannot be 6' 5". Most of us will never run the four-minute mile, or become Miss America, or win an Olympic medal. Most of us never will be famous, or beautiful, or ingenious. We cannot control the law of gravity. We cannot call back cruel words already spoken. We cannot change our past. We cannot change the aging process. And we cannot eliminate death.

I could go on and on, pointing out numerous things in our lives which we cannot change. The real question is, How do we respond to those "trees" in the midst of our garden? Some people spend their lives running away from them. That's what the one-talent servant did. He tried to run away. He hid the money to escape the pressure.

Some people play the "if only" game. If only I were taller; if only I were smarter; if only I were richer; if only I had married someone else; if only I had gone to a different college; if only I had that house, or that car, or that job; if only I had more than one talent. But, you see, the "if only" game doesn't work. It only causes us to fail to face reality, and it leads to bitterness, misery, and self-pity. The Christian answer is the serenity of acceptance—even, indeed, the redemption of our handicaps.

This is what Jesus was doing in the Garden of Gethsemane when he prayed, "Father, if this [cup] cannot pass unless I drink it, your will be done" (Matt. 26:42). That is the serenity of acceptance.

Sure, the last servant had less than the other two, but he had enough. He had enough to do something positive and meaningful and productive. But because he would not accept what he had, he did nothing. I wonder how often that happens to us. He failed, first, because he didn't appreciate what he had, and second, because he didn't accept what he had.

He Didn't Use What He Had

The servant didn't try at all. He hid his talent in the ground.

While we were in Dallas, our son Jeff had a business meeting at South Fork Ranch, the place where they made the long-running TV series *Dallas*. South Fork has been turned into a tourist attraction and convention center, and Jeff was impressed by how beautiful the ranch is. He wanted us to see it, so one evening after dinner we drove out there. We only intended to drive by the front, but when we got there, we saw tour buses and people everywhere. Off in the distance from the road, we saw a hundred people or so in and around the ranch house. The sign on the gate said, "Tours 10:00 A.M. to 5:00 P.M.," and even though it was 7:30 P.M., we saw all those people up there—in the house, on the balcony, by the pool, in the backyard—so we ventured toward the front door of South Fork. When we got up there, somebody said, "You know, this might be a private party." But one person in our group (who shall remain forever nameless) said, "Well, let's give it a try. If it's a private party, we can just blend in for a few minutes, take a quick look, and then slip out."

When we walked in the front door, we noticed something immediately: Everybody there had on a blue bandanna. Everybody there had on a big name-tag. Everybody there was from Japan! Quick thinkers that we are, we realized immediately that it was indeed a private party and that we were going to have a hard time blending in. But then the hostess came over to us. We confessed that we had sort of stumbled in, and she said, "Oh, that's okay. We are so glad that you are here. Come on in and let me show you around." She gave us the VIP tour, and even took our picture. It was a wonderful experience.

Now, please don't misunderstand me; I'm not urging us to crash private parties. I am simply saying that when we venture forward and try, when we appreciate and accept and use what we have, then great things can happen. On the other hand, if we give up on life, if we pull back into a hard shell, if we vegetate in apathy, if we live in fear, if we refuse to risk, if we refuse to try, then nothing good is going to happen for us or come our way.

The point is clear: Don't wait; do it now. If you have a word of love that needs to be expressed, say it now. If you have a broken relationship that ought to be fixed, go fix it. Don't let the sun go down tonight without setting it right. If you have a commitment you need to make, there is no better time than now. If you have been thinking about joining the church, don't wait a minute longer. Do it today. If you have something you need to be doing, seize the moment. Do it now.

In a backdoor sort of way, we learn from this parable of the talents a helpful and sensible formula for victorious living, namely this: Appreciate what you have, accept what you have, and, with the help of God, use what you have. DON'T QUIT. Keep on trying.

Remember That

CHRISTIANITY IS A LIFE WE LIVE, NOT JUST A CREED WE PROFESS

Scripture: Micah 6:6-8

ing Duncan and Angela Akers in their book *Amusing Grace* (Knoxville: Seven Worlds, 1993) have recorded a fascinating list of humorous answers given by middle school students on their examination papers. Here are some of the interesting answers:

The people who follow the Lord were called the Twelve Opossums.

The spinal column is a long bunch of bones. The head sits on the top and you sit on the bottom.

Henry VIII, by his own efforts, increased the population of England by 40,000.

The blood circulates in the body by flowing down one leg and up the other.

The death of Francis Macomber was a big turning point in his life.

It is so hot in some parts of the world that the inhabitants there have to live somewhere else.

The wind is like the air, only pushier.

In order to have different seasons we had to get the earth tilted over on its axis, but it has been worth it.

Meteorologists look something like people.

You can listen to the thunder after lightning and tell how close you came to getting hit. If you don't hear it, you got hit, so never mind.

A list like that reminds us that right answers are important, but—have you thought about this?—so are right questions. With that in mind, I want to raise in this chapter what I think is a right question that each of us needs to grapple with personally: What in the world does God want from me?

Some years ago a young man home from college asked that question in my office, and as he spoke, I could hear anguish in his voice. He was having a rough time of it. He was trying to find himself. With his newfound freedom on the college campus, he had experimented with several different pretty bizarre lifestyles (which he described to me in lurid detail), but admitted that none of that had been fulfilling. He still felt empty and lost inside.

"So," he said, "I turned to religion." The truth is, he dabbled around the edges of several different religious approaches, but nothing he tried had brought peace to his troubled soul.

Finally, he said, "I must be going about this all wrong. I'm doing lots of religious things, but God doesn't seem impressed. I'm lighting candles. I'm burning incense. I'm wearing love beads. I've tried fasting and chanting and meditation, but still, I don't feel very close to God."

He paused for a moment; then, with a painful expression, he said, "What in the world does God want from me?"

What would you have said to that young man? How would you have responded to his sincere question?

This young man and I talked for a long time about a number of things. We talked about Christ—the life, the teachings, the death, the resurrection of Jesus Christ—the salvation and abundant life that are available to us through him, and what that means to us today. We talked about grace, that we don't have to win God's love; it is freely given. Our part is to accept it, celebrate it, and share it with others. We talked about commitment, that Christianity is not just a creed we profess, not just rituals we perform; it's a lifestyle we live daily. We also talked about the fact that he was not the first to raise this significant question.

As a matter of fact, when that young man cried out, "What in the world does God want from me?" I immediately thought of this powerful passage in the book of Micah that is our text for this chapter. Micah 6:6-8 is without question one of the Bible's best moments, one of the highest mountain peaks in all of the Scriptures.

"With what shall I come before the LORD? (What does God want from me?) Shall I bring him burnt offerings or animal sacrifices? Will the Lord be pleased with lavish displays, thousands of rams, or ten thousands of rivers of oil? Shall I sacrifice my firstborn child, the fruit of my body for the sin of my soul?" (vv. 6-7 paraphrased).

Is that what God wants?

Does he want animal sacrifices? No. Does he want human sacrifice? Of course not. Well, what is the answer? What in the world does God want from us? What pleases him most? Here is the prophet Micah's classic response: All God wants is for us "to do justice, and to love kindness, and to walk humbly with [our] God" (v. 8).

That's all. With those three powerful phrases, Micah takes us as high as the Old Testament can take us. He sees clearly that much of the religion of his day had got off track. The people were doing religious things like lighting candles and burning incense and offering sacrifices, but it was having no impact on how they lived daily. They were going right out of the Temple to cheat people in the marketplace. They had a form of religion, but it was not a force in their daily lives. So, Micah writes these strong words to bring us back to the light—back to the major thoroughfares of faith. Let's look at these three powerful statements.

God Wants Us to Do Justice

The noun and verb here are both important. We are to *do justice.* It's not enough to want justice. It's not enough to talk about it, or dream about it, or wish for it. God wants us to do justice, to work for justice in our world. The word *justice* in the Scriptures means "righteousness," and it's a two-edged sword. It means doing right personally and working for what is right in our society.

Several years ago in Ohio, the backdoor of an armored truck came open on an interstate highway. Two million dollars flew out the back. Can you imagine? It was something; people went crazy. It was raining hundred-dollar bills on that interstate highway.

Motorists were gleefully stopping and grabbing

the money, stuffing it into bags and sacks and into their clothing, and then speeding away. One man, a repairman, picked up $57,000. The reason I know the exact amount is because he turned it in the next day. He said he couldn't sleep; it wasn't his money, and he couldn't keep it in good conscience. He was one of a very few who felt that way.

Of the $2 million lost, a very small percentage of it was returned, and most of that by this one man.

The response of his parents was interesting. His father said, "What? He gave it back? I thought my son was smarter than that. I didn't do a very good job raising that boy. He must have a screw loose. He gave it back? How stupid can you get?"

But, on the other hand, his mother said, with a warm, gentle smile, "We needed the money. We sure could have put it to good use, but I'm so proud of him. It was the right thing to do."

That's what it means to do justice. It means to do the right thing personally. But that's not enough. We also have to work for justice for others in our society. Whenever people are hurting or abused, whenever people are mistreated or oppressed, our calling is to be there for justice, working for rightness.

If you remember the decade of the 1960s, you

might remember a powerful folk song made popular by Peter, Paul & Mary, "If I Had a Hammer." The song speaks of hammering out justice, working for freedom, and cultivating love all over the land. That's what God wants from us. What pleases God most is to see God's children standing up for one another and hammering out justice for all people in this world; to see us, God's children, standing tall for what is right. God wants us to do justice.

God Wants Us to Love Kindness

Joseph Telushkin has written a powerful book about the ethics of speech. It's called *Words That Hurt, Words That Heal: How to Choose Words Wisely and Well* (New York: William Morrow and Company, 1996).

Over the past decade, Telushkin has conducted workshops throughout the country on the powerful (and often negative) impact of words. During his workshops, he does an interesting thing. It's a bit blunt, but it surely does make the point. He asks his audiences if they can go for twenty-four hours without saying any unkind words about or to anybody. The responses of people are revealing. A few of the people will raise their hands signifying that, yes, they can do that. Many of the people will respond to the question by just laughing nervously. But quite a large number will shout out, "No!"

Telushkin then says candidly, "Those of you who can't answer 'yes' must recognize that you have a serious problem. If you cannot go for twenty-four hours without drinking liquor, you are addicted to alcohol. If you cannot go for twenty-four hours without smoking, you are addicted to nicotine. Similarly, if you cannot go for twenty-four hours without saying unkind words about others, then you have lost control over your tongue" (Telushkin, "Words that Hurt, Words that Heal," *Imprimis* [journal of Hillsdale College in Michigan], January 1996).

Telushkin goes on to challenge the workshop participants to monitor their conversation for two days. He asks them to note on a piece of paper every time they do an unkind deed or say a negative or unkind word over that two-day period. He goes on to point out that most people who honestly take that test are unpleasantly surprised.

Oh, how important it is that we in the church learn how to cultivate the attitude of loving-kindness. Our kindness may be the only sermon some person out there will ever hear. As Christians, we are called to imitate the kindness of our Lord. One of my favorite poems expresses it like this:

"What is the real good?"
I asked in musing mood.
Order, said the law court;
Knowledge, said the school;
Truth, said the wise man;
Pleasure, said the fool;
Love, said the maiden;
Beauty, said the page;
Freedom, said the dreamer;
Home, said the sage;
Fame, said the soldier;
Equity, said the seer; —

Spake my heart full sadly,
"The answer is not here."

Then within my bosom
Softly this I heard:
"Each heart holds the secret;
Kindness is the word."
(John Boyle O'Reilly, "What Is Good?")

What does the Lord require of us? What in the world does God want from us? To do justice, and to love kindness, and, third and finally, this:

God Wants Us to Walk Humbly with Our God

When I was quite a bit younger I preached a sermon on that powerful text from Isaiah 40 that says, "[We] shall mount up with wings like eagles,

125

[we] shall run and not be weary, [we] shall walk and not faint" (v. 31).

In the sermon, I mentioned that this verse mystified me because it seemed out of sync, that it should be turned around—that we should walk, then run, and then fly.

After the sermon, a good friend named Marian, who was in her eighties at the time and who was one of the greatest saints I ever knew, came to me and—as she always did in her gracious, humble way—complimented me on my sermon.

Then she said, "Jim, I'll tell you why that verse in Isaiah 40 bothers you. It's because you are still young. When you get older, you will understand it and appreciate it.

"You see," she said, "Isaiah was right. That's the way it works in the faith pilgrimage. You fly, you run, you walk. When you first have a faith experience, you are so excited you want to fly like an eagle. Then you settle back after awhile and run with perseverance like a marathoner. But the real test of faith is the test of time and endurance, that daily humble walk with God. That's what it's all about."

Now that I am older, I understand what she was talking about. She and Isaiah were, indeed, both right. As someone once put it: It's not how loud you shout, it's not how high you jump; it's how you walk when you hit the ground.

What does God want from us? Simply this: To do justice, to love kindness, and to walk humbly with our God.

Epilogue

You Can Be So Near, But Yet So Far

Scripture: Mark 10:17-22

 few years ago, a young Catholic priest finished his seminary training and was appointed to serve a church in Loveland, Colorado. He was so excited to begin his ministry. On his first Sunday there, he looked out the window of his study and was thrilled to see so many people driving into the parking lot. The cars were lined up back-to-back.

"Wow," he said out loud, "we're going to have a packed house today!"

However, just a few minutes later, when he walked into the sanctuary to begin the Mass, he was stunned to see that there were only fifteen or twenty people sitting in the pews. He was concerned, disappointed, and mystified by this. Where were all of those people? All of those cars were pouring into the parking lot just moments ago, but where were the people?

Amazingly, the next Sunday the same thing happened. A lot of people drove into the parking lot, got out of their cars, came around to the entrance of the church, and entered the front door. Yet when the priest stepped into the sanctuary to start the Mass, only a handful of people were there.

On the third Sunday, the young priest decided to get to the bottom of this. So instead of peering out the window toward the parking lot, he went around and positioned himself where he could discreetly see the entrance to the church. Immediately the mystery was solved. Sure enough, the people were driving into the parking lot in large numbers. Sure enough, they were getting out of their cars, and they were coming around and entering the front door of the church. However, instead of coming all the way into the church and taking their place in the pews, these people were stepping in just far enough to dip their fingers in the holy water and make the sign of the cross, but then they would scurry out of the church, get back into their cars, and drive off to other pursuits.

Now, think about that—the picture of people coming in just far enough to get the holy water.

It's a vivid parable for our own time because every church has a similar problem. That is, we have people who come into the church just far enough to get a kind of sprinkling of religion, people who come into the outer edges of the church to receive a blessing or to be on the rolls, but not far enough to give their hearts and souls to the cause of Christ.

They want the church to be here; they want the church to serve; they want the church to have good programs, a good staff, nice facilities, and plenty of parking; and they are quite anxious for the church to help them in their time of need; but really they want to keep God at arm's length. They don't want to get too close, too involved, too interested, too committed. They just want to come far enough in to get a little holy water every now and then, just a little sprinkling of religion, then it's off to the cars and off to other interests. They are so near, but yet so far.

Now, this shallow, "so near, but yet so far" approach is not a new phenomenon; it's as old as the Bible itself. We see it graphically in Mark 10. The rich young ruler is the prime example of "holy water religion," of "so near, but yet so far" faith. He knows that the answer is in Jesus Christ, but he is not willing to go with Jesus all the way. He's just playing around the edges of Christianity.

He walks up to the door, but he won't go completely in. He wants to question, but not to follow. He wants to converse, but not to commit. He wants to "talk the talk" but not "walk the walk." He wants to play with the holy water, but not to live a holy life.

When Jesus says to him, "Get your priorities straight and come and follow me" (v. 21 paraphrased), the rich young ruler heads for the parking lot. When Jesus says to him, "Come, follow me; come, be one of my disciples; give me your loyalty, your prayers, your presence, your gifts, and your service," the ruler turns away, saying in effect with his body language, "I didn't want to get into it that much. I didn't want to be that serious about it. I thought I might give my left hand to it, but not my life. I just wanted to dab my hands in the holy water a little bit; I didn't want to give my heart and soul to it."

When it comes to following Christ, the rich young ruler is like so many people in our time: so near, but yet so far. So, with that in mind, let me ask you a question: Aren't you tired of being so near, but yet so far? What are you waiting for? Why don't you come all the way in? Won't you come all the way into the church, all the way into discipleship, all the way into Christianity? Let me be more specific with these three thoughts:

Come All the Way into Faith

Don't stop too soon. Don't stay out there on the fringe. Don't play around the edges of faith. Come all the way into the Christian faith—heart, mind, soul, and strength. Do the best you can and trust God to bring it out right. Give your life to God and trust God completely.

Too often we are like the man who fell off a cliff. As he tumbled, he caught hold of the branch of a small tree. There he hung between heaven above and the rocks a thousand feet below. He knew his strength was giving out and that he wouldn't be able to hold on long. In desperation, he looked toward heaven and shouted, "Is there anybody up there?"

No response. Silence. He tried again: "O Lord, are you up there? If you are up there, Lord, please save me. Spare me, Lord, if you are up there, and I will believe in you and have faith in you and serve you all my days. If you are up there, Lord, please deliver me and I will be your faithful servant for the rest of my life."

Imagine the man's surprise when this booming voice came back at him from above: "Oh, sure you will; that's what they all say when they're in trouble."

"Not me, Lord," the man answered back. "I'm different from the rest. Now that I know for sure that you are up there, I will have total faith in you. I will trust you unreservedly. I will obey you completely."

"Okay," the Lord said, "I will save you right now. Just trust me and let go of the branch."

The man then asked, "Is there anybody else up there?"

Isn't that precisely what we do? We come close to God; but then when God calls on us to trust him and do something we don't really want to do, we turn away, looking for something else more convenient to put our faith in. That is exactly what the rich young ruler did that day. He couldn't trust. He couldn't obey. He couldn't follow. He couldn't let go of the branch of his riches. He turned away, looking for something easier, something more comfortable, something less demanding. He turned away saying, "Is there anybody else up there?"

Now, with all the feeling I have in my heart, let me tell you something: There isn't anybody else up there. God is the one and only Lord of life. Our calling is the same as that given to the rich young ruler long ago: Get your priorities straight. Get your loyalties straight. Get your life in order. Let go of whatever branch is holding you back. Accept God, and trust, obey, and follow him. Make that leap of faith, and you will have treasure in heaven. Don't hang out on the edges; don't be so near, but yet so far. Come all the way into the Christian faith.

Come All the Way into Commitment

All of us are familiar with the Salvation Army. Especially at Christmastime we see their volunteers in front of stores, dressed in uniforms, ringing their bells and collecting money to help needy people. The Salvation Army does the thankless kind of work that many folks don't really want to do. They reach out with love and grace to help the poor, the hungry, the homeless.

The Salvation Army was started many years ago in London by a devout Christian named William Booth. Today, it's a worldwide organization. Their mission is simply to help poor people in the name and spirit of Jesus Christ, to give the love of Christ to needy people.

But how did that ministry get started? What was going on in General Booth's life to inspire such an undertaking? Well, actually someone asked General Booth that very question, and his answer was powerful. He simply said that God had all there was of him. He said there had been people with greater brains and greater opportunities, but when he caught a vision of what Jesus Christ could do with him and the poor of London, he made up his mind that day that Jesus Christ would have all of William Booth there was. He went on to say that if there was anything of power in the Salvation Army it was because God had all the adoration of his heart, all the power of his will, and all the influence of his life.

That's what Christian commitment is—giving our all to God. That's what the rich young ruler was unable to do, and sadly that's what many of us are unwilling to do. Let me ask you something: Can you say what William Booth said, that God has all there is of you—all the adoration of your heart, all the power of your will, and all the influence of your life? Can you say that? Are you that committed? Are you?

Will you take a step in that direction today? Will you commit your heart and soul and mind and strength to Christ? Will you accept him, follow him, obey him, and serve him? Don't hang out on the edges. Don't play around in the shallow water. Don't be so near, but yet so far. Come all the way into faith, and come all the way into commitment.

Come All the Way into Love

There's an old story about the man who landed a job with the highway department painting the yellow line down the center of the highway. This he had to do by hand.

After three days, the foreman called him in and said, "Your first day out, you did great. You painted that line for three miles. Your second day wasn't bad. You painted two miles. But today you only painted one mile. I hate to do it, but your work has slacked off so much that I have no choice but to fire you."

On his way out of the office, the worker looked back over his shoulder and said, "It wasn't my fault. Every day I got farther away from the paint can."

One thing is sure in the Christian faith: the farther we get away from love, the farther we get away from Christ. Jesus himself put it like this: "A new commandment I give to you, that you love one another; as I have loved you. . . . By this all will know that you are my disciples, if you have love for one another" (John 13:34-35 NKJV).

A woman visited a newspaper editor's office one morning hoping to sell some poems she had written. "What are your poems about?" the editor asked. "They're about love," gushed the poet. "Well, read me one," said the editor. "This world could certainly use a lot more love."

The poem she read was filled with starlight and roses and other sticky sentiments, and it was more than the crusty old editor could take. "I'm sorry," he said, "but in all honesty, you are really missing the boat on what real love is all about. It's not moonlight and roses. It's sitting up all night at a sickbed, or working extra hours so the kids can have new shoes. The world doesn't need poetic love. It needs some good old-fashioned, practical love."

Jesus showed us that on a cross.

Once there was a little four-year-old girl who knew nothing about Christ and his church. She had never heard the stories of Jesus. Her parents were not interested in the church at all, so they never took her.

But one day her uncle came to visit. He was a devout Christian and a great churchman, and out of respect for him and his faith, the parents asked him to pray at mealtimes.

The little girl was fascinated. The uncle realized that, so he told her about Jesus and taught her how to pray to God, how to bow her head and close her eyes and put her little hands together reverently in front of her and talk to God and thank him for all of her blessings. All went beautifully and the little girl loved it.

But then one evening the uncle left and went back to his home. The next morning the little girl rushed to the breakfast table. She climbed into her chair. She bowed her head, closed her eyes, positioned her hands, and waited for someone to say the prayer thanking God for the food and the new day, but all she heard was the tinkling of silverware and the crinkling of the morning paper as her mom and dad rushed through breakfast. Confused, she opened her eyes and said, "Mommy, Daddy, isn't there a God today?"

Let me ask you something: Can people tell by the way you live and the way you love that there is a God today?

The call of Jesus is to deep faith, deep commitment, deep love. The rich young ruler was so near, but yet so far. Please don't let that happen to you. Come all the way in.

STUDY GUIDE

THE TOP TEN LIST FOR CHRISTIANS

Written by Sally D. Sharpe

This study guide is designed for both individual and group use. When using the book individually, you may choose to read the entire book and then revisit each chapter as you make your way through the study guide. Or, if you prefer, you may take one chapter at a time, reading a chapter and then considering the questions provided for that chapter. In either case, you will find it helpful to record your responses and reflections in a notebook or journal.

When using the book in a group, you may cover one chapter per session, or you may combine or select specific chapters as you choose to shorten your study. When combining two or more chapters for a given session, you may condense the material by selecting from the study questions provided. (Note: The study questions provided for the Epilogue are to be used in a time of personal reflection, prayer, and commitment. They are not intended for group use.)

Prior to your first session, determine who will serve as group leader. For this study, the leader's role is to facilitate discussion and encourage participation by all group members. To ensure fruitful discussion, *all participants* must commit to reading the designated chapter(s) before each group session. If open discussion is new or uncomfortable to your group, or if your time together is limited, it may be helpful for group members to reflect on the selected study questions prior to the session as well. Some may want to record their responses in a notebook or make brief notes in their books. (Note: Some questions may seem more appropriate for personal reflection than for group discussion. If members of your group are reluctant to discuss these questions, agree to reflect on them individually during the coming week.)

Remember, this is a study *guide*—intended to help lead you on an exploration of the book's primary themes and lessons. The "journey," however, will be different for each group or individual making it. Some will need to take a few detours; others will want to linger at times before moving ahead. Whether studying the book alone or with a group, feel free to adapt the questions as necessary to meet your particular needs and interests or those of your group. In addition to this book, you will need a Bible and a Bible concordance. Though it is not essential to your study, you may also find a Bible dictionary to be a helpful resource. (Groups will need only one Bible concordance and one Bible dictionary.)

May God richly bless you through your study.

Number 10: *Remember That* Love Is the Greatest!

1. Read 1 Corinthians 13 in its entirety. How is your understanding or appreciation of the often-quoted "Love Chapter" affected by the author's description of the context in which the apostle Paul was writing (see pages 13–16)? In what ways are we Christians today similar to the Corinthian Christians? What kinds of specific problems threaten to tear apart the church universal, the body of Christ? your own local church and/or denomination?

2. The thirteenth chapter of 1 Corinthians explains the "more excellent way" that Paul writes of in the last verse of chapter 12; this more excellent way is the way of love. What does it mean to live the life of love, to make love your aim, to put love first in your life? If possible, give an example from the life of someone you know who has made love the number one priority of his or her life.

3. Do you agree with the old saying that gratitude is the parent of all other virtues? Why or why not? Reflect on/discuss the following statement: It's our gratitude that produces our faith, our hope, and our love.

4. Read Colossians 3:14-17. What can we learn from these verses about love and gratitude? Verse 17 instructs us to "do everything in the name of the Lord Jesus, giving thanks to God the Father through him." What does this mean? Give a specific example from your own life or the life of someone you know, if possible.

5. What worries do you have about the future—your own future as well as the futures of those you love?

List some of these worries, on your own or as a group. Now read Matthew 6:25-34. What do these verses instruct you to do? What assurance or promise does Jesus give in verses 32 and 33? What, if anything, is keeping you from living "one day at a time"?

6. Read Psalm 118:24. What changes would others see in your life if you followed the advice of this verse *each day*? We've all heard the saying *carpe diem*—seize the day. As Christians, how are we called to "seize the day"? How are we to live each day to its fullest? Briefly tell about someone you know who truly rejoices in every day.

7. Read 1 Thessalonians 5:16-18. What does it mean to "rejoice always" and to "give thanks in all circumstances"? Do you believe this is actually possible? Why or why not? Does giving thanks *in* all circumstances mean the same as giving thanks *for* all circumstances? Explain your answer.

8. How would you define *graciousness*? List as many synonyms for the word as you can. Are the words *gentleness* or *gentle* on your list? Read the following Scripture verses: Matthew 11:29; Colossians 4:6; 1 Thessalonians 2:7; Titus 3:1-2; and 1 Peter 3:4. What do these verses tell us about the ways we are to be gracious and gentle to others?

9. Think of a time when your view of a person or situation changed instantly after you learned about that person's "hidden pain." What did you do? In retrospect, what would you have done differently? How does viewing others compassionately, rather than making assumptions or jumping to conclusions, help us to be more loving and gracious?

144

10. How did Christ exemplify love rooted in graciousness? Scan one or more of the Gospels to find as many supporting examples as you can.

11. How is generosity more than giving of our money and material possessions? What does it mean to be generous in our relationships with others? Give an example from your own life or the life of someone you know, if possible.

12. Read Romans 12:10. What do you think this verse means? In what ways is Paul encouraging us to be generous?

13. Read the following statements: Love leads to gratitude, graciousness, and generosity. Gratitude, graciousness, and generosity lead to love. Do you agree with either statement, or with both statements? Why? Give an example from your own life or the life of someone you know to support your answer, if possible.

14. Reread 1 Corinthians 13:13. What do you think Paul means here? How would you rewrite this verse in your own words?

15. The author writes that love is the key sign of Christian discipleship. How did Jesus teach and live this truth? Cite specific stories or scripture passages to support your response, if possible. How have you experienced the truth that "love is the greatest" in your own life?

Number 9: *Remember That* Hope Is Still Alive

1. Read Luke 24:13-35. Christ walked with Cleopas and Simon down the road to Emmaus, but they did not recognize him until later that evening,

145

while they were breaking bread together. Sometimes we too are unaware of Christ's presence with us. Can you think of a difficult period in your life when you were blind to Christ's presence with you until sometime later? If so, what eventually "opened your eyes"? As you look back now, in what ways can you see that Christ was with you?

2. Other times when we are hurting, we are acutely aware of Christ's presence with us throughout the experience. Can you think of such a time in your own life? If so, how did you know that Christ was with you? In what ways was he with you as never before during this difficult time?

3. Read Psalm 30. Have you ever been able to say with the psalmist David, "You have turned my mourning into dancing; you have taken off my sackcloth and clothed me with joy" (v. 11)? Think of a time when God turned your sorrow into joy, your despair into hope, your disappointment or defeat into victory. How did you respond? In what ways did you offer your thanks and praise to God? Respond to/discuss this statement: Praise is a natural and necessary response to God's healing work in our lives.

4. The author names several "holy habits" through which we experience the healing power of Christ in our lives: prayer, Bible study, the Sacraments, involvement in a body of believers (the church), and a daily walk with Christ. How have these holy habits helped you to experience Christ's healing power in your own life? Do you think any of the habits is more important than the others, or are all equally important to our spiritual health?

146

Why? At times when you have become "lazy" in one or more of these habits, what has happened?

5. What other "habits" help you draw closer to God? What helps you to experience Christ's healing presence?

6. Reread the story about Charlie Brown and Peppermint Patty on pages 30 and 31. How would *you* answer Peppermint Patty's question: "What do you think security is?" Respond to/discuss this statement: The good news of the Christian faith is that we have someone to hold our hand.

7. Read John 4:7-14 and 1 Peter 1:3. In these verses we read about "living water" and "living hope." What do these phrases mean? What do these verses tell us about resurrection and eternal life?

8. In what ways are we "resurrected" when we experience and accept the risen Christ? What are some of the evidences of this new life in Christ?

Number 8: *Remember That* Faith Has Its Own Taste Test!

1. Read Psalm 34:8. In your own words, explain what it means to *taste* the Lord's goodness. What does it mean to receive God *within*? In what ways have you personally *experienced* God in your life?

2. According to one meaning in *The American Heritage Dictionary* (3d ed., 1992), to *redeem* is to rescue or ransom. Read the following Scripture verses: Romans 3:23-24; Ephesians 1:7; and Colossians 1:13-14. Drawing upon these verses, how would you revise or expand the definition of *redemption* as it relates to the Christian faith?

147

Your definition should tell *what* we are saved from as well as *how* we are saved.

3. Read Ephesians 2:8-9. What role does grace play in our redemption? In what way is God's grace a gift, freely given?

4. One of the results of our redemption, our salvation, is that we are changed; our lives are made over, turned around. For some, the changes are immediate and dramatic. For others, the changes are gradual and more subtle—yet just as significant. Give an example—from your own life, or from the life of someone you know or someone you have heard of or read about—to illustrate both ways God works in the lives of those who accept the free gift of salvation.

5. Read Acts 10:39-43 and 1 John 1:9. What two things must we do in order to receive God's forgiveness?

6. Read Matthew 18:21-35. What does this story teach us about forgiveness? (See also Matt. 6:14-15; Mark 11:25; Luke 6:37; and Col. 3:13.)

7. In what way is forgiveness a "cycle"? Respond to/discuss this statement: Because God forgives our sins, we should joyfully forgive others.

8. Read Romans 15:4-5. God encourages us, through God's amazing grace, in so many ways. As we read in this passage from Romans, one of the primary ways God encourages us is through the Scriptures. In what other ways have you tasted the encouraging love of God? In other words, how has God mended your heart, lifted your spirit, renewed your hope, and restored your energy for living?

9. Read Acts 20:1-2 and 1 Thessalonians 5:11, 14. As members of the body of Christ, why is it impor-

tant for us to encourage one another? When and how have you been encouraged by your brothers and sisters in Christ? What are some other ways we may encourage one another?

Number 7: *Remember That* It Matters Intensely What You Believe

1. What are some of the popular or "trendy" religious ideas and appeals vying for our attention today? In what ways, if any, are these ideas and appeals *similar* to the Christian faith? In what ways are they *different*?
2. How would you define a *cult*? How would you explain the difference between a cult and a healthy faith?
3. Respond to/discuss this statement: Religion is like a parachute; it works best when open. What is an "open" faith? What does it mean to be open to new truths from God?
4. Do you believe it is possible to be open to new ideas without sacrificing tradition? Why or why not?
5. Read Luke 9:28-36. What was Peter's temptation? What was wrong with Peter's desire? Have you ever had a spiritual "mountaintop experience" that you didn't want to end? Looking back now, how have you grown in faith since that experience? What made that growth possible?
6. What are some of the ways we can be intentional about growing in our faith? What have you found to be most productive in your own life?
7. Have you ever known anyone whose faith was nothing more than an "insurance policy" for heav-

en? What was missing from this person's faith? Now think of someone whose faith is a vital, integral part of his or her daily life. How would you compare and contrast the lives of the two individuals? (Omit names if sharing with a group.)

8. Read Matthew 5:13-16. In what ways are we, as Christians, called to be the "salt" of the earth and the "light" of the world? When we fail to be the salt of the earth and the light of the world, what happens—to the world as well as to ourselves?

9. According to Matthew 7:26-27, what happens when we fail to put our faith into action? Now read James 1:25. What does this verse tell us will happen when we act on our beliefs? Ask yourself: Am I a *hearer* only, or am I also a *doer*?

10. Read John 13:34-35. What does it mean to love others as Christ loves us? How would you rewrite these verses for someone unfamiliar with the Christian faith and the life of Jesus Christ?

11. Read 1 Corinthians 13. Respond to/discuss this statement: Love should be the primary distinguishing characteristic of a Christian. As Christians, how should our love be different from the world's understanding of love?

12. Read Matthew 22:37-39. In what way do these two "greatest commandments" encompass both the devotional life and spiritual action?

13. Review the three different approaches to religion discussed on page 55. Why are the first two approaches incomplete and ineffective? Why are both worship and service necessary for a healthy, effective faith? What are some ways we can balance the two in our day-to-day lives?

14. Respond to/discuss this statement: Jesus Christ is the Christian's measuring stick.

Number 6: *Remember That* God Is Smarter Than You Are

1. Read Matthew 6:9-11 and Matthew 26:36-39. What theme do these two prayers have in common? Why is it important for us to pray for God's will to be done? What does praying in this way require of us?
2. Can you think of a time in your life when you were "in the garden of Gethsemane"—a time when you prayed for something difficult or painful to pass you by? If so, what were the circumstances of your life then? What did you hope would happen? Were you able to pray for God's will to be done, regardless of the outcome? Why or why not? What actually happened? Looking back now, can you see God's will in the turn of events?
3. Why are trust and humility necessary ingredients for effective prayer? What can we do to keep our prayers from becoming arrogant "wish lists"? How can we cultivate a spirit of complete trust in our prayer life?
4. Respond to/discuss this statement: Prayer doesn't always change our circumstances, but it always changes us.
5. What does it mean to "have the mind of Christ" (1 Cor. 2:16)? Read 1 Corinthians 3:9-16. What does Paul tell us in these verses about having the mind of Christ? What does the Spirit of God do for us? (See 1 Cor. 2:6-16.)
6. In your own words, define *Christian obedience.*

Reread page 65. What are some ways we can "condition, train, and prepare ourselves to obey God in every circumstance and . . . apply God's will to every situation"?

7. To put God's will above our own requires complete and unshakable commitment. Jesus is the supreme example of this kind of commitment. What other individuals in the Bible, in the pages of history, and/or in your own life come to mind when you think of those who are totally committed to God? What are the evidences of each person's commitment to God?

8. Respond to/discuss this statement: Commitment to God is not a one-time decision but a never-ending succession of decisions.

9. On a scale of 1 to 10, with 10 being the highest, how committed are you to God *right now*? Answer as honestly as you can. If this is difficult for you, ask yourself: Have I surrendered every area of my life to God in complete trust and humility? Am I obedient to God in every circumstance of my life each and every day? Consider what you can do to increase your commitment to God today.

Number 5: *Remember That* Every Now and Then We All Hear a Rooster Crow

1. How would you define the word *profane*? *The American Heritage Dictionary* (3d ed., 1992) offers these definitions and synonyms: blasphemous; nonreligious, secular; vulgar. Unfortunately, there are examples of profane language and behavior all around us. How often have you seen or heard pro-

fanity—in word or action—this week? Did you respond in any way? If so, how?

2. The author suggests six reasons people use profane language: ignorance, insecurity, anger, a desire to be accepted, insensitivity, and to "let off steam." What are some other possible reasons people swear? Do you think any of these are "legitimate" or acceptable reasons for using profane language? Why or why not?

3. Do you agree with the belief that *strong* language is sometimes necessary, such as at times of extreme provocation, though such language does not have to be *vulgar*? Why or why not?

4. Read Mark 14:65-72. Why do you think Peter cursed and swore an oath before denying Jesus for the third time? What effect do you think Peter's words had on the crowd?

5. What guidelines does the Bible give us regarding the use of God's name? Look at Exodus 20:7 and Deuteronomy 5:11. Use a Bible concordance to locate other specific passages. Respond to/discuss this statement: No situation ever justifies using the name of God in a curse or oath.

6. In his book *Look at the Burning Bushes,* Robert Goodrich writes: "It's quite possible to be pious in language, proper in words, and profane in attitudes." It is easy to recognize when words are profane, but how can our *attitudes* also be profane?

7. On page 75, the author names some attitudes that are profane. What other attitudes would you add to the list?

8. Respond to/discuss this statement: Any attitude or action that hurts, dehumanizes, depersonalizes, or

treats others with contempt or disrespect is profane.

9. With the previous definition in mind, what kind of profane attitudes or actions have you seen, heard, or committed recently? What were the results of those attitudes or actions? What can be done now, if anything, to right the wrongs of those attitudes or actions?

10. What can you do to discourage and counteract profane words, attitudes, and actions
    in your own life?
    in your family and circle of friends?
    in the place where you work?
    in your neighborhood or community?
    in the body of Christ?
    in society at large?

Number 4: *Remember That* You Don't Have to Cross the Fox River Until You Get to It

1. We're all guilty of inventing fears, magnifying problems, and exaggerating potential threats. Give an example from your own life of a time when you allowed unnecessary worry to cause you great anxiety. What happened? If you could relive the experience, what would you do differently?

2. The gospel message is clear: God is with us and will see us through every situation. Why, then, do you think we worry so much? Why is it so difficult for us to "let go and let God," as the popular saying goes?

3. There are numerous passages in the Gospels in which we hear and see Jesus responding to the

fears of the disciples—and many others. Again and again Jesus assures them that there is no need to fear; he is with them. All they need to do is have faith. Two such passages deal with storms at sea. Read Matthew 8:23-27 and Matthew 14:22-33. Then answer the following questions:

- What were the disciples afraid of?
- How did Jesus respond to their fear(s)?
  What did he say?
  What did he do?
- What did the disciples then say and/or do?

What do these stories teach us about worry and faith?

4. Do you agree that fear is sometimes helpful or *constructive*? If so, give an example from your own life. If not, explain why.
5. When is fear *destructive*? What does this kind of fear do to us? Give an example from your own life, if possible.
6. Read John 14:27. How can these words help to allay our fears when the storms of life are raging around us? What does Jesus promise us?
7. Have you ever felt far from God? What were you afraid of at that time in your life? What eventually restored your trust and your hope? Were you later able to see that you had been in the palm of God's loving hand all along? If so, what brought you to this realization? If not, spend some time in prayerful reflection and consider how God was working in your life even then.

155

8. Reread Matthew 14:27-30. In what ways are you like Peter? What spiritual desire or goal do you have at this time in your life? What fears do you have that are related to this desire or goal? What "step of faith" is God calling you to take?

9. What does it mean to "celebrate life"? Quickly and spontaneously make a list of ways we can celebrate life—seize it, taste it, experience it, savor it, share it, and thank God for it—each and every day. Now, in the same manner, make a list of common fears, behaviors, or attitudes that often prevent us from celebrating life in these ways. What can we do to anticipate and overcome these negative "joy-squelchers"?

10. In Matthew 14, we learn that even the disciples were afraid of death. If we're honest, *all* of us have some kind of fear or anxiety related to death and dying. What are your fears? Read Romans 8:35-39. How do these verses speak to your fears? What specific promises do they hold for all believers? (See also John 3:16; 5:24; 6:40; and 14:1-3.)

Number 3: *Remember That* There Are Some Roads We Just Don't Need to Go Up

1. Read 1 Thessalonians 5:16-22. How does giving thanks in all circumstances—living in the spirit of gratitude—keep us from wandering down the dangerous "roads" of life? Give an example from your own life or the life of someone you know, if possible.

2. How does living *without* gratitude "quench the Spirit" within us (see v. 19)?

3. The author writes that selfishness is a threat to the

156

soul (see page 100). What happens to us when we become selfish and self-centered? Give an example from your own life or the life of someone you know, if possible.

4. Read John 12:25; John 13:34-35; and Luke 6:27-38. What did Jesus teach us about *selfless* love versus *selfish* love? What happens to us when we shift our focus from serving ourselves to serving others? What does self-giving love help us to discover?

5. Think of a time when you voluntarily and joyfully helped another person—without any desire for praise, appreciation, or reward. How did helping this person make you feel? What did you learn from the experience? What was your so-called "reward"?

6. How does pride destroy the spirit of gratitude within us? In what way is pride rebellion against God? Use a Bible concordance to find passages that warn against *pride*. What lessons do these Scriptures hold for us?

7. The opposite of pride is humility. If pride is rebellion against God, what, then, is humility? Why do you think God desires a humble spirit? Read James 4:10 and 1 Peter 5:6. What do these verses tell us God does to those who are humble? Explain your answer.

8. Read Philippians 2:5-11. In what way was Jesus the ultimate example of humility? What did Jesus teach about humility? See Matthew 18:1-4; 23:12; Mark 9:35; Luke 14:7-11; 18:9-14.

9. Gratitude or thanksgiving is a common theme in the apostle Paul's Letters. Why do you think this is

so? How is gratitude a key sign of the Christian faith?

10. How is *ingratitude* incompatible or inconsistent with the Christian faith? Read 1 Corinthians 15:57 and 2 Corinthians 9:15. What victory is ours through Jesus Christ? What "indescribable gift" has God given us?

11. Read Psalm 145:10 and Psalm 150:6. How are gratitude and praise related? What are some of your favorite ways to express your gratitude to God through praise?

12. Paul not only instructs us to give thanks to God; he also instructs us to encourage and build up one another (1 Thess. 5:11). What are some of the ways we can do this? How does expressing gratitude help to "build up" another?

13. Think of a time recently when you expressed your gratitude to someone—with a simple "thank you" or some other gesture of appreciation. How did the individual respond? How did this make you feel? How are we to respond when others ignore or rudely "reject" our expressions of gratitude? Share an example from your own experience, if possible.

Number 2: *Remember That* You Do Better When You Try

1. Read Matthew 25:14-29. What is the moral or lesson of this parable? Read also Luke 12:36-48. How is the lesson of this parable similar to that of the parable of the talents? What does God expect of us as "faithful servants"? What can we do to meet these expectations?

158

2. Reread Matthew 25:24-25. Why did the third slave hide his master's money? What prevented him from being trustworthy?

3. When has fear prevented you from trying? Of what were you afraid? In what ways did your fear keep you from being faithful or trustworthy—to yourself, to others, or to God?

4. Read Mark 5:36. In your own words, explain what this verse means. Do you believe that we are able to overcome all fear through faith? Why or why not?

5. What is *apathy*? Do you believe that everyone who does not try, who "quits on life," is apathetic? Why or why not? When and how does apathy lead to failure? Respond to/discuss this statement: Refusing to try is the perfect formula for failure.

6. What happens when we compare ourselves to others who have more than we do? How does ingratitude discourage, disable, and defeat us? Give an example from your own life or the life of someone you know, if possible.

7. Respond to/discuss this statement: The riches of life are all around us, but so often our eyes fail to see them for the simple reason that we magnify the difficulties, overlook the advantages, and fail to see the good in what we have. Tell of a time when *you* magnified the difficulties, overlooked the advantages, and/or failed to see the good in what you have. What happened?

8. Why do you think it is so difficult for us to accept life's limitations? What limitations have been difficult for you to accept in your own life? How have you responded to these limitations?

9. The author suggests that when we are faced with lim-

159

itations, we generally respond in one of three ways. Describe each of these responses or choices (see page 113). Which is the appropriate response for the Christian, and why? What does it mean to "redeem our handicaps"? Give an example from your own life or the life of someone you know, if possible.

10. Read Luke 22:41-44. Jesus was in such anguish as he prayed in the garden of Gethsemane that "his sweat became like great drops of blood" (v. 44). He was experiencing tremendous inner turmoil, yet the author writes that Jesus demonstrated the "serenity of acceptance." How so? What can we learn from Jesus' example?

11. Take a careful look at yourself and your life. How have you been blessed by God? Has God given you a special ability, talent, skill, possession, or something else that, for whatever reason, you have not put to use? If so, why have you been reluctant to use this/these gifts? What can you do to put this/these gifts to use for God's glory?

12. Read Matthew 25:1-13. How are we like the foolish bridesmaids in this parable when we do not try—when we do not use what God has given us? Why is it important that we appreciate, accept, and use *right now* what God has so graciously given us?

Number 1: *Remember That* Christianity Is a Life We Live, Not Just a Creed We Profess

1. Respond to/discuss this statement: Christianity is not just a creed we profess, not just rituals we perform; it's a lifestyle we live daily. How would you

describe or explain the way we are called to live as Christians?

2. Read Micah 6:6-8. According to Micah, what does God want from us? How would you rewrite verse 8 for contemporary readers? In addition to the requirements mentioned in verse 8, what else does God want from you in your life?

3. The author describes how the people of Micah's day had allowed their religion to become a meaningless ritual, a lifeless routine. In what ways are we guilty of the same thing today? Is there evidence to suggest there is a need for spiritual renewal in the church universal? in your congregation? in your own life? If so, give examples. Is there evidence to suggest spiritual renewal is already taking place in the church universal? in your congregation? in your own life? If so, give examples.

4. Read Proverbs 21:3. What does this mean? How does it affirm the prophet's words in Micah 6:8?

5. Read the following Scripture verses: Deuteronomy 10:17-18; Psalm 37:28; Psalm 103; Psalm 140:12-13; and Psalm 146:5-9. What do these verses tell us about God's justice? about the recipients of God's justice?

6. Injustice and oppression deprive others of their basic needs or rights. To *do justice,* then, is to correct those wrongs and meet those needs. Yet a biblical understanding of justice takes it one step further. Read Psalm 107 and Psalm 113:7-9. How do these verses show that God's idea of justice not only involves meeting needs and righting wrongs but also bringing about complete restoration?

161

How are we called to participate in God's plan of restoration? What are some of the ways *you* can help to bring about justice and restoration in your community and beyond?

7. When we think of doing justice, we tend to think of working on behalf of others. How is doing justice also a personal matter? In what ways can we "do justice" in our own lives?

8. Respond to/discuss this statement made by Joseph Telushkin: "If you cannot go for twenty-four hours without saying unkind words about others, then you have lost control over your tongue" (see page 124). Consider accepting Telushkin's challenge to monitor your conversation for two days, noting on a piece of paper every time you do an unkind deed or say a negative or unkind word.

9. What does the author mean when he writes, "Our kindness may be the only sermon some person out there will ever hear"?

10. Read John 13:34. Jesus not only instructed us to love one another, to be kind to one another; he also showed us *how* by his example. What Gospel stories would you share with someone unfamiliar with the life of Jesus to illustrate his kindness and love? (Choose the first stories that come to mind.) What are some ways we can model Jesus' kindness and love in our own lives? Give one or more specific examples, if possible.

11. What does it mean to "walk humbly with God"? Describe someone you know or have known who has or has had this kind of relationship with God.

12. Why is it important not only that we walk with

God daily, but also that we *walk humbly*? Read
Isaiah 57:15; Matthew 11:29; 18:4; 23:12. What do
these verses tell us about our need for a humble
spirit?
13. In biblical and contemporary language, the term
walk often refers to one's relationship with Christ
and/or the way one lives out his or her faith. Read
the following Scripture verses: Romans 6:4;
Romans 8:4; 2 Corinthians 5:7; 1 John 1:7; 1 John
2:6; 2 John 6; 3 John 3-4. What insights do these
verses give us regarding the way we are to "walk"
as Christians?

Epilogue: You Can Be So Near, But Yet So Far

Note: The following questions are to be used in a time
of personal reflection, prayer, and commitment. They
are not intended for group use.
1. Read Mark 10:17-22. Try to imagine yourself in the
place of the rich young ruler. You've just met Jesus,
and you've asked him what you must do to inherit
eternal life. How does he respond to you? What "one
thing" do you lack? What does Jesus ask you to do?
2. Read Psalms 52:8; 62:5-8. David, who is credited
with writing these verses, put his trust in God
again and again; as a result, he experienced first-
hand God's never-ending love and faithfulness.
Consider the way David describes our God:

- God is steadfast, faithful.
- God's love endures forever.
- God is our rock, our salvation, our fortress, our
deliverer, our refuge.

- God is always trustworthy; God will never let us down.
- God cares about us and is always ready to listen.
- God loves and accepts us as no one else can.

According to David's experience, what happens when we trust our God?

- We are filled with hope.
- We are strengthened.
- We are delivered.
- We are honored.
- We are sheltered, protected.
- We are saved from destruction.
- We are nurtured and nourished.
- We are tenderly and lovingly cared for.

No wonder David implores us to "trust in [God] at all times" (Ps. 62:8). *Do you?* If not, what fears are keeping you from trusting God completely? Read and meditate on the following psalms: 23; 90; 118. Claim their promises. Put your trust in God. God *will* be faithful!

3. Read Mark 12:30. Now reread the verse, replacing the word *love* with the words *commit yourself to.* That is what real commitment to God is—devoting your heart, mind, soul, and strength to God. Are you that committed to God? Have you committed your heart, mind, soul, and strength to Jesus Christ? Perhaps you once did, but now you need to recommit your life—your all—to Christ. Ask yourself, What is keeping me from *total commitment*? Be honest with yourself and with God. Then sur-

render to God whatever is holding you back, and ask God to take *all* of you.

4. Reflect on this statement: The farther we get away from love, the farther we get away from Christ. How far away from love are you right now? Or, to put it another way, how much closer to the love of Christ would you like to be? Meditate on John 13:34-35. How is God calling you to change? What is God calling you to do? How will you respond?